74788

£20

Nigel Colborn's

GARDEN
MAGIC

Nigel Colborn's

GARDEN
MAGIC

Successful planting by numbers

First published in 1998 by

Quadrille Publishing Limited

Alhambra House, 27-31 Charing Cross Road,

London WC2H 7AT

Art editor: Mary Staples

Project editor: Carole McGlynn

Editor: Jackie Matthews

Picture research: Nadine Bazar

Production manager: Candida Jackson

Illustrations by Lynne Robinson and Richard Lowther

Special photography by Georgia Glynn Smith

British Library Cataloguing-in-Publication Data
A catalogue record for this book is available from the British Library.

ISBN 1 899988 08 4

Printed by KHL Printing Co Pte Ltd

half-title page:
Dramatic in drifts and beautiful in close-up, a white
form of Himalayan balsam (*Impatiens glandulifera*).

title page:
Late-summer morning mist over a display of Welsh
leeks (*Allium sphaerocephalon*) and phlox.

page 4:
North American coneflowers (*Rudbeckia*).

page 5:
Ornamental garlics (*Allium caeruleum*) are almost as
beautiful in bud as in bloom.

Contents

► Successful planting results in a long-lasting display that sustains interest as it changes through the season. Here, an ice plant (*Sedum spectablile*) has been teamed with marjoram.

Good planting can make or break a garden. However brilliant and inspired a garden design may be, ultimate success will depend upon the plants used, and on how well they are arranged. Every garden needs architecture, of course, so that the space is put to optimum aesthetic and practical use, but good planting will always be a prerequisite for lasting enjoyment, and, moreover, for that special pleasure which is generated by a constantly changing pattern, month by month and season by season.

To be effective, any planting must echo at least some aspects of the natural landscape. This does not mean that a faithful imitation is required, but that the various key components which make up natural vegetation should be present in every garden. These components, which encompass aesthetics, structure and colour, are discussed in the first part of this book. Their successful interaction is illustrated by a series of planting schemes in the central section of the book, each recipe having been drawn from a finely designed, well-planted garden. Seasonal continuity and difficult garden situations are explored in the last part of the book.

The art

of planting

MAKING CHOICES

Planting is an essential ingredient of garden design, but rather than merely making general selections we need to compose arrangements and companion plantings that, together, make a far bigger impact than the simple sum of the parts. We are lucky to have at our disposal a bewildering array of exciting plants, drawn from every corner of the globe. Whatever effect is desired – be it formal or naturalistic, simple or complex – there will always be a comprehensive choice of plants which will provide all the necessary elements, not only in terms of shape, size and colour but also in terms of more subtle constituents such as texture, fragrance and character.

Ground rules

The whole concept of creative planting is underpinned by three simple rules. The first is that plants must be suited to their environment; only healthy plants will provide a good display, so it is essential to choose species and varieties that will thrive, naturally, in their alloted space. The second rule is that the gardener must be happy with the plants and the way they are arranged; only grow plants that you personally enjoy, in arrangements that you are happy with. Finally, the plants must be combined to achieve the most pleasing associations, not only of colour, but of shape, texture, outline and character; it soon becomes obvious which plants look good together.

With more than 100,000 different kinds of plant in cultivation worldwide, these rules are easily followed, and any site that can support life is a potential garden. However hostile an environment might be, however poor the soil, however harsh the climate, there are bound to be varieties that will cope. But rather than merely choosing species that will survive, it is important to select plants that will thrive and look their best. Thus, even if you live in a semi-desert — as a surprisingly large number of people do, around the world — your choice will almost certainly run to plants that are adapted to those special conditions. But as the world carries a vast desert and semi-desert flora, this is not a limiting factor.

In a virtually frost-free garden you can leave tender species to develop year on year, but even in a cold climate the choice is never restricted. For example, when you consider how many gorgeous flowers appear on the summer prairies of North America or in the Caucasus, both of which suffer horrendous winters, and when you see what gems can bloom close to the snow line in the Himalayas, the Rockies or the Andes, then it becomes clear that the whole world is a garden, and that the essence of planting is simply to assemble the most pleasing combination of plants.

▶ Some planting opportunities are easily overlooked. Even the arid environment at the base of a large tree, furnished as here with poor soil, can be turned to advantage. This collection of succulents has created a delightful evergreen display in a wide range of hues.

▼ Towering in the foreground, the giant oat (*Stipa gigantea*) makes a strong structural statement. At ground level, mat-forming plants soften the hard edges of the paving as well as bring the area to life. Through the seasons, the paving always looks the same, but natural plant growth ensures a constantly changing picture.

When planting a new garden or area, your first task, from a practical point of view, is to assess the habitat. Familiarize yourself with local soil types, average temperatures and rainfall, especially the winter and summer extremes. A general idea will do: summer heat waves exceeding, say, 30°C (86°F), will be too hot for such cool-climate plants as European primroses and Himalayan poppies. If temperatures dip to 0°C (32°F) or below, tender plants will not survive outdoors.

One of the simplest ways of gathering valuable data about your garden is to observe what the neighbours are growing, not necessarily to mimic what they do, but to see what kinds of plant thrive for them, and to make sure at least some of these feature in your design.

If you want to make an exception with some special favourites, grow them in containers, where the right conditions – special winter protection, perhaps, or different soil – can be provided. For instance, if your soil is strongly alkaline, you will have to grow lime-hating plants such as camellias or citrus trees in tubs filled with ericaceous compost; if it is acid, be prepared to lime your kitchen garden.

▲ A naturalistic display of prairie annuals and perennials demonstrates two of the rules for successful planting: that plants should adapt happily to their surroundings and associate comfortably with one another. Much of the colour here comes from North American godetias, supported by such members of the daisy family as gaillardias and white-flowered mayweed (*Anthemis cotula*).

Plant outline

Good outline plants

Erect

Carpinus betulus 'Fastigiata'

Fagus sylvatica 'Dawyck' and 'Dawyck Purple'

Ilex aquifolium 'Green Pillar'

Prunus 'Umineko'

Tiered

Cornus alternifolia

Cornus controversa

Magnolia x *loebneri* 'Merrill'

Viburnum plicatum

Conical

Abies koreana

Picea omorika

Picea pungens

Every plant has its own special characteristics, such as type of foliage (pages 12–13), flower (pages 14–15), colour (pages 16–17), even scent (page 18–19), but a distinctive shape is what makes certain plants eminently more suitable for creative planting than others.

Some outline features are obvious at a glance: ask anyone to draw a tree, and they will usually present you with a sketch of a broadly rounded crown rising from a trunk. A shrub will be similar, but with its roundness resting directly on the ground. This is over-simplistic, of course, for trees can be tall and thin, like a Lombardy poplar or the holly *Ilex aquifolium* 'Green Pillar'; or they can be conical, like spruces and firs; or, loveliest of all, they may carry branches which are tiered in layers, as seen in *Cornus controversa* or, on a smaller scale, *Viburnum plicatum*. These shapes, in all their subtle variations, are extremely valuable for creative planting.

With plants other than trees or shrubs, the most prominent outline feature might be huge leaves, as seen in the ornamental rhubarbs (*Rheum*) or the mighty foliage of *Gunnera manicata*. Or it could be curiously twisted branches, as in the corkscrew hazel (*Corylus avellana* 'Contorta') or the willow *Salix babylonica* var. *pekinensis* 'Tortuosa' (syn. *S. matsudana* 'Tortuosa'). The way in which the flowers are presented often makes a plant's outline particularly attractive: the tubular blooms of foxgloves, all pointing in the same direction, the unmistakable spikes of mulleins

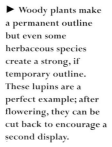

▶ **Woody plants make a permanent outline but even some herbaceous species create a strong, if temporary outline. These lupins are a perfect example; after flowering, they can be cut back to encourage a second display.**

◄ Outline plants vary in shape from tall, thin and erect, through weeping, to rounded. One of the most valuable shrubs is *Viburnum plicatum*. Not only are its branches arranged in stately tiers, but when the flowers appear in early summer, they are arranged in perfect rows all along the upper surface of each branch, accentuating the layered shape.

(see An Aromatic Gravel Garden, pages 54–57), the long, elegant catkins of the North American evergreen *Garrya elliptica* and the metre-long racemes of the Japanese wisteria *W. floribunda* 'Multijuga' (syn. *W. japonica* 'Macrobotrys') are a few diverse examples.

It is possible to generalize growth habits into tall or short, compact or spreading, coarse or refined and so on. Within those categories, every plant has its own special combination of characteristics which extends the range of variations to an almost limitless number. It is at this level that the difference between a perfect choice and a near miss can be made when selecting a plant for a particular position. Suppose, for example, that you were looking for a plant with a neat, rounded dome shape. There are plenty to choose from. Many genistas produce the desired shape, as do cotton lavenders if they are regularly dead-headed, though eventually the latter tend to collapse. Box, some hollies, yew and privet,

which can all be sculpted into shape by regular clipping, are also candidates. However, the Mediterranean wild shrub *Daphne sericea* Collina Group (syn. *D. collina*) grows naturally into an almost perfect evergreen hemisphere seldom more than 50cm (20in) across, and in late spring and early summer it is smothered with intensely fragrant, purplish-pink flowers. In the right conditions – sunny, alkaline and not too moist – this plant is the indisputable correct choice for providing exactly the required outline.

The same process of elimination should be employed for every other shape. Indeed, it is often more helpful when selecting plants to think first about shapes in abstract terms. For example, rather than say to yourself, 'I'd like a rose for that corner' or 'a cherry tree would be perfect on that part of my lawn', think in terms of a general shape and then, once you have decided exactly what sort of outline you want, choose a plant to fit.

▲ *Rheum palmatum* towers above tulips and forget-me-nots, creating the impression of a solid, almost monumental structure. Though herbaceous, this architectural plant will preside over the area from mid-spring until summer's end.

Foliage

► The broad, felty foliage of a sage (*Salvia argentea*) contrasts with the spiky leaves of rosemary to make a rich blend of leaf textures and shapes. The dark purplish sage leaves provide a colour contrast to the silvery hue which is echoed in the helichrysum.

Plants with outstanding foliage
▼

Acer palmatum var. *dissectum* (purple or green)

Cercis canadensis 'Forest Pansy' (purple)

Cotinus coggygria 'Royal Purple' (purple)

Cotinus 'Grace' (purple)

Hedera colchica 'Sulphur Heart' (lime-green and green)

Philadelphus coronarius 'Aurea' (gold)

Physocarpus opulifolius 'Diabolo' (dark purple to black)

Veratrum nigrum (green)

Veratrum viride (green)

Vitis vinifera 'Purpurea' (purple)

As the biggest contributor of plant material, in both volume and style, foliage is as important in successful creative planting as flower (pages 14–15). Most good plant associations use a composition of foliage either to create a strong, supporting background for the flowers or to develop a leafy display in its own right. Indeed, in many plantings flowers play a subordinate role to leaves, as illustrated in A Shady Urban Oasis (pages 94–97) and in An Arid Planting (pages 90–93).

Every leaf has a unique set of characteristics, which contribute to its value as a decorative element in creative planting. The soft, feathery foliage of tamarisk and fennel gives an airy-fairy effect, the antithesis of bergenias, whose broad, rounded leaves have the texture of polished leather. Evergreens can be dull and forbidding, but the leaves of such plants as camellias, hollies and some of the laurels have a sparkling 'wet look' due to the waxy cuticles. They look wonderful on their own but are even better with something flowering amongst them.

The colour, texture and often the shape of leaves changes constantly through the seasons. Evergreens produce soft, vibrant new growth, and in such conifers as blue spruce (*Picea pungens*) this is an exquisite and unique shade of blue-grey. In high summer, golden and variegated leaves tend to lose their intensity and turn greener, but usually return to bright gold before falling. Even dark purplish leaves, such as those of the lovely *Cotinus coggygria* 'Royal Purple' or the purple vine (*Vitis vinifera* 'Purpurea'), progress through a succession of changes throughout their lives. Fern leaves uncurl as they grow, creating a unique 'fiddle-head' shape before they mature.

To emphasize the character of individual plants, try placing them with others that have contrasting foliage. Nothing sets off featheriness better, for example, than a broad, heavy leaf. Thus, the lacy leaves of the Japanese maple (*Acer palmatum* var. *dissectum*) make a softening contrast with the leathery solidity of bergenias, perhaps, or the bold, pleated foliage of Indian poke (*Veratrum viride*) growing beneath them. A lasting popular association, aided because both plants enjoy similar growing conditions, is to combine moisture-loving ferns with hostas: the broad, plantain-like leaves of the hostas are a perfect complement to the fussy, feathery fronds of the ferns.

◀ When plants with different types of foliage are placed together, exciting contrasts in both colour and texture occur. Here, the freshness and softness of a fern (*Matteuccia struthiopteris*) is accentuated by the silvery leaves of an ornamental deadnettle (*Lamium maculatum* 'White Nancy'). Though pretty, flowers would be unnecessary in this delightful planting.

▶ The leaves on the slender, straight twigs of *Cotinus coggygria* run through a sequence of colours from fresh spring green through an autumnal process, when they become suffused with red and gold before falling. This effect can be enhanced if the shrub is pruned hard each spring.

Flower

It would be hard to imagine a garden totally devoid of flowers, though such gardens do exist. Even those classic Chinese gardens that show nothing but leaf in summer will have an abundance of blossom in spring. And in the greenest of green Western gardens, flowers are used, albeit sparingly, to create focal points of colour. Moreover, since flowering plants are abundant in almost every natural habitat, it follows that a garden without flowers would tend to look unnatural.

How you use flowers in your garden will depend on what kind of effect you want to achieve, but whatever the planting style certain factors need to be borne in mind.

Large, brightly coloured blooms are so conspicuous that they always will be noticed as individuals wherever they appear. If used with discretion this is an advantage, but if such plants are wrongly placed problems can soon result. A single tree paeony bearing huge papery blooms, for example, creates a superb focal point, weekend wonder though it may be. But a whole bed of large-flowered dahlias or chrysanthemums in many colours delivers a visual shock rather than a joyous impact, and is unlikely to sit easily in its surroundings.

Depending on how they are used, dense concentrations of bloom, even if the individual flowers are quite small, can be as effective, or as uncomfortable, as a bed of large flowers. A drift of bright azaleas, for instance, blooming beneath emerging, golden-green foliage in a spring woodland garden would please most tastes, as would a moorland carpet of purple

► Contrasting colours are achieved here by combining the vivid gold foliage of the common hop (*Humulus lupulus* 'Aureus') with a blood-red climbing rose (*Rosa* 'Frensham'). The dark foliage of the rose adds a further dimension, emphasizing the brightness of the hop leaves. Allowing different climbers to intertwine provides a huge range of potential contrasts in colour, texture and form, as well as a blend of fragrances.

Flowers for misty sprays

◀ The coral-pink hue of this opium poppy (*Papaver somniferum*) almost clashes with the orange suffusions in the antirrhinum, but the effect is lively and dramatic – perfect for a well-lit spot.

Ajania pacifica

Cimicifugas (rat-tails)

Crambe cordifolia

Gypsophilas

Lobelia richardsonii

Macleayas

Nemesia caerulea

Persicaria amplexicaulis

Thalictrum delavayi

◀ A lazy, misty late-summer effect has been achieved in this meadow planting by allowing grasses to set seed without cutting back. Colour comes as much from the dried bodies of flowers that have matured as from newly opened blooms. There are still plenty of fresh flowers to come, particularly with the ox-eye daisies, which will extend the season well beyond the middle of summer.

heather in full bloom or a lilac-blue wisteria in full flower against an old mellow brick wall. A bed of orange French marigolds, however, planted so densely that their blooms are almost touching and growing next to an equal-sized bed of scarlet salvias would make anyone feel restless. Whether that is good or bad is a matter of personal taste.

It is more difficult to harmonize the colours of large flowers than of small ones. Colour clashes show up more obviously and any nearby plant bearing blooms that are smaller or in subtler colours will tend to disappear.

Conversely, borders or plantings that contain large numbers of very small flowers can employ all sorts of colours, even ones that jar, without spoiling the effect as long as they are sited close together. As an example, compare a typical flower meadow with the dahlia bed described above. In the dahlia bed, crimson will shout at scarlet, which will look nasty with peach and sit extremely uncomfortably next to certain shades of blush pink. But out in the meadow, yellow buttercups, pink ragged robin, blue speedwell, white cow parsley, scarlet poppies, purple knapweeds and rusty sheep sorrel will all blend happily together, creating a gentle mottling of brilliant colours.

The more densely flowers are planted, the harder it is to appreciate their individual characteristics. This can be a disadvantage, particularly with such distinctively shaped blooms as irises, lilies or gladioli. A single specimen or a small, loose group will show off the shapes of the flowers rather better.

Large plants that carry sprays of tiny flowers, such as gypsophila, thalictrum or the dramatic *Crambe cordifolia*, create a vast but diffuse, misty effect, often softening distant views rather than blotting them out.

Lower, creeping diascias and aubrietas or such flattened shrublets as thymes and sun roses (helianthemums) can be planted in dense groups to develop mats of colour when they are in flower, and green ground covers when they are not. In some respects, these can be compared with painting, that is using carpets of flower or leaf as surface covers to develop patches or drifts of colour.

Some flowers are as important for their ground-covering abilities as for their three-dimensional display. Penstemons, for instance, provide conspicuous patches of colour and last for the entire growing season, but, seen close to, their handsome tube-shaped blooms carry subtle markings in their throats.

Colour

Colour is as important in foliage as in flower, and although green is the predominant colour in most gardens, it is a common misconception to assume that foliage colours are always more muted and more subtle than flowers.

In foliage plants colours can be loud, among variegated forms especially, making judicious placing essential. The yellow and green of the variegated holly *Ilex × altaclerensis* 'Golden King', a female despite its masculine name, for example, are so strident that the plant becomes a focal point wherever it is sited. In winter this is terrific, but care is needed when choosing its companions for summer. A good general rule with variegated plants is to avoid positioning any two closely together, since they will almost always create a discordant colour combination.

Purples, bronzes and golds are common hues among foliage, and provide a superb soft palette for creating gentle colour pictures, with or without flowers. As with variegated

▶ Foliage and flower work harmoniously here, with clean, bright blue lesser periwinkle (*Vinca minor*) flowers set off by the sombre, purplish suffusions in the leaves of *Bergenia cordifolia*. Both plants are evergreen, so the foliage effect will continue through the year, but with subtle changes of hue.

▶ A dwarf maple (*Acer palmatum*) fires up for a final display before its leaves fall to make a russet carpet at its feet. Such trees have immense year-round value: in spring and summer their hues can range from golden-green to sombre purple, depending on the variety.

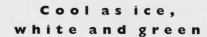

Cool as ice, white and green

◄ Gardeners' garters (*Phalaris arundinacea*) with white wood cranesbill (*Geranium sylvaticum* 'Album').

The white parallel striping along the leaves of the grass enable it to play 'straight man' to the pretty five-petalled flowers of the cranesbill. This simple plant combination works perfectly, even when the geranium flowers are over and only the sculpted leaves remain to contrast with the grass.

Plants' special needs

Phalaris arundinacea is an invasive grass with a creeping rootstock, so be sure to plant it only where it can be controlled. The roots will run and run, whether the soil is rich or impoverished. The cranesbill is rather short-lived in bloom, but will often flower again if the stems are cut back as soon as the first flush has faded. Equally happy in sun or semi-shade, wood cranesbill performs best if it is lifted and divided every three years.

Others to try

Holcus mollis, a slightly less troublesome grass, is also green and white, but has narrower, softer leaves. In very full sun, on poorer soils, try substituting the white form of meadow cranesbill (*Geranium pratense* f. *albiflorum*) or perhaps the lower-growing albino bloody cranesbill (*G. sanguineum* 'Album').

Off-season echoes

In spring, *Brunnera* 'Hadspen Cream' has cream and green foliage with pale blue flowers, but for a whiter white, both in leaf and flower, try white-variegated honesty (*Lunaria annua* 'Alba Variegata') and enjoy the autumn bonus of its lovely translucent seed capsules.

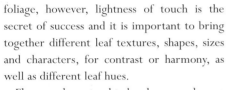

foliage, however, lightness of touch is the secret of success and it is important to bring together different leaf textures, shapes, sizes and characters, for contrast or harmony, as well as different leaf hues.

Flower colours tend to be cleaner and more intense than those of leaves. Their bright hues are designed to attract pollinating agents — usually insects, though birds, bats and even mice pollinate some species — and the fact that we humans can also be drawn to them is no more than a happy accident.

Plants that are pollinated by night-moving agents often have paler hues than those visited during the day, enabling them to stand out in the twilight. When selecting plants for a scheme, it is always worth including a number of very pale pastel shades and plenty of white, if you want the planting to continue to look attractive in failing light. Hotter or harder colours — vivid reds, oranges, peacock blue or bright purple — will show up less in poor light conditions, but when they are energized by strong sunlight, they will appear almost to pulsate with colour.

The creative use of colour in planting schemes is discussed on pages 44–51.

Additional benefits

In addition to the more obvious attributes of shape, flower colour, character and so on, every shrewdly chosen plant will boast other benefits. Fragrance, autumn colour, winter outline and even the quality of young leaves, for example, are all valuable bonuses that will boost a creative planting plan.

Ensuring maximum fragrance is one of the most important, and yet most neglected aspects of creative planting. Everyone understands that some flowers smell pleasant, and some herbs are fun to pluck at and sniff, but how much careful composition goes on to ensure a pleasing blend of aromas? Did you know, for example, that lovely as honeysuckle and roses are for individual fragrance, the blend of their perfumes together on a warm summer night is one of the most sensual outdoor experiences? And when you know that sage, marjoram, lavender and rosemary all give off their aromas most effectively when they are heated by sunlight bouncing off a stone or brick surface, you understand why they are ideal as pathside plants. To widen the dimensions of the plantings, fragrant species

▲ Two plants provide constant delight as a simple group at the edge of a lawn. The rhododendron is evergreen, with vivid spring colour. The foliage of the Japanese maple continues to be beautiful after it has fallen to the ground.

▶ Plants with bonus displays are always the most valuable. The rounded seedheads of *Allium cristophii* are nearly as lovely among dying grasses as the purple flowers were amid spring greenery.

are included in almost all of the plant recipes featured on pages 52–131.

Autumn colour is another very desirable attribute. As well as the sought-after reds and russets, there are yellows, as exhibited by members of the birch tribe, the rich tan of maturing purple beech leaves or even the buff parchment hue of dead hornbeam leaves.

The outline of plants in autumn and winter can be as important as their glorious summer flowers. The advantages of some plants, like conifers or clipped evergreens, are obvious,

pristine newness for so short a time, as the American poet Robert Frost observed:

> *Nature's first green is gold*
> *Her hardest hue to hold.*

Beyond the golden-green shades of most new leaves there are some special plants: the salmon-pink leaf buds of *Acer pseudoplatanus* 'Brilliantissimum'; the richer pink and cream of the young leaves of the buckeye *Aesculus ×neglecta* 'Erythroblastos' and the little silvery-white candles of the whitebeam *Sorbus aria* 'Lutescens'.

We must consider, too, the importance of a garden's ecology, and the wildlife it harbours. Gardens can be refuges for a wide range of species without our having to compromise on beauty or design. Where there is an option, choose wildlife-friendly species: nectar-rich plants for bees and butterflies; plenty of berry-bearing and seed-bearing plants for birds during winter; lots of thick ground cover and climbing plants, such as ivy, which provide winter shelter for so many species. And where there is water, it is important to plant so that the aquatic habitat can support as much diversity as possible. Oxygenating plants will keep the water sweet enough for dragonfly nymphs and caddis larvae; floating leaves, such as those of water lilies and water hawthorn, will provide cooling shade in high summer, and a generous planting of marginals will give shelter, not only to birds and animals coming to the pond or stream to drink, but also to such creatures as tiny young frogs and dragonfly nymphs which are emerging from the water to take up adult life.

All these additional attributes have to be considered when selecting plants. Indeed, it is important to subject every potential plant choice to a set of challenging entry requirements, which should begin with the question: 'what will you contribute to my garden when you are not flowering?' If the plant you are questioning is unable to give you a straight answer, select something else!

but more subtle displays such as glossy bark, found on the trunk of the Chinese cherry *Prunus serrula*, or sticky horse chestnut buds, or even dead seedheads on perennials also have their value. Fruits, including berries, the fluffy, bearded seeds of clematis, and the old

skeletons of fennel, looking like ruined fairy umbrellas, are glorious in autumn. And when these are frost-rimed or covered with a light dusting of snow, their charm is captivating.

Emerging foliage is almost always lovely, part of its value being because it retains its

Practical attributes

As no-one wants a garden to become a source of disappointment and since the aim is for all the plants in a planting scheme to thrive, it makes sense to select for vigour, and for the overwhelming majority of the plants to be easy to grow. After all, the loveliest plants on earth are of little value unless they are at least reasonably endowed with practical attributes.

Although pests and diseases are common everywhere in the world, there are sufficient resistant, robust plants available to render chemical pest control almost unnecessary. Species or garden forms of plants that are close to their wild forebears are usually more vigorous than highly bred garden forms.

Where disease is concerned, however, some genera are high-risk plants. Roses suffer the most, especially highly bred varieties, so if you grow them you will need either to be very selective or to spray regularly with fungicide. Perennial asters, particularly those raised from *A. novi-belgii*, goldenrods (*Solidago*) and bergamot (*Monarda*) are all prone to mildew and need regular spraying with fungicide to keep them clean. Most other perennials are fairly healthy, if managed correctly.

Hardiness is an important consideration where winters are cold. There is nothing wrong with growing tender species in frost zones, but you need to be aware of the danger of loss, and to provide winter protection where necessary, or to be ready to replant each spring. Most frost-tender perennials are

simplicity itself to propagate and then to over-winter under glass with minimal protection.

Because propagation is a chore – great fun, but very time consuming – varieties that tend to replicate themselves without becoming a nuisance will always be popular. From such boisterously promiscuous annuals as the Californian poppies (*Eschscholzia*) and the pot marigolds (*Calendula officinalis*) to the more cherished oriental hellebores, say, or wild Turkish tulips, self-seeding plants are a joy. The natural, relaxed appearance of several of the planting recipes shown in this book (pages 52–131), result from allowing many of the plants to self-seed.

Self-supporting plants are less trouble than those that need training, staking or tying. Obviously, climbers and certain architectural plants are so valuable that they are worth the extra individual attention they need, but among perennials, those that stand on their own are much less trouble than lanky plants which flop in the slightest breeze. Thus, border pinks, which need no support, are preferable to the similar border carnations which often do. With shrubs, those that grow to a convenient size and shape with minimal attention are preferable to those that need regular pruning, or that tend to grow coarse with advancing years.

Some species are more demanding than others, of course, and any really enthusiastic gardener will want to rise to the challenge of

bringing tricky varieties to perfection. If you are determined to raise difficult plants, concentrate on those that are so gorgeous, they are worth the extra trouble. For example, some people find lilies difficult, and almost everyone struggles with those wonderful blue Himalayan poppies (*Meconopsis betonicifolia*), but if you can succeed, the results are so rewarding that they are worth the effort.

As every plant must pay its rent, it is important always to insist on the very best examples of the plants you have chosen to grow – the healthiest, the best coloured and the neatest or most charming in growth habit.

▶ Gardening is always made simpler by selecting plants that are easy to grow and need minimal attention. Opium poppies (*Papaver somniferum*), in seed here, and love-in-a-mist (*Nigella*) are annuals which replicate themselves freely and yet seldom become a nuisance. Both are almost as attractive when gone to seed as in flower. They are totally frost-hardy, and will stand without support.

Planting styles

A wild meadow-like effect

▶ *Tulipa sprengeri* naturalized among *Anthemis punctata* ssp. *cupaniana*.

Wild tulips will always make a dashing focal point. The vivid scarlet *Tulipa sprengeri* is among the last of the tulips to bloom and its open flowers have straw-coloured petal backs, making them even more dramatic. There is a wide choice of daisy-like marguerites available: *Anthemis punctata* ssp. *cupaniana* has silver, feathery foliage but is not reliably hardy in cold areas. A tougher alternative would be the European ox-eye daisy (*Leucanthemum vulgare*), whose blooms are almost indistinguishable from those of anthemis.

Plants' special needs

The tulips will naturalize from both seedlings and running stolons. Though happy in full sun, they reproduce more readily if their bulbs are allowed to grow in ground that does not dry out too much in summer. If the marguerites are cut hard back in mid-summer, they will regenerate a second flush.

Others to try

For an earlier, similar effect blend vivid red *Anemone × fulgens* or the multi-headed *Tulipa praestans* with cool, green-flowered euphorbias or the black widow iris (*Hermodactylus tuberosus*). Doronicums make splendid spring displays of yellow daisy flowers, admirably set off by such hybrid tulips as red 'Apeldoorn' or purple 'Negrita'.

Off-season echoes

With the right choice – argyranthemums, leucanthemums or anthemis – the daisy theme will run and run. Supporting plants could be changed by placing lilac colchicums among the tulips for autumn colour.

The choice of possible planting styles is almost without limit. Any gardener who admires the gracious parterres and courtyards of the seventeenth century will probably want a neatly ordered, symmetrical planting in their garden. A genuine nature-lover or country-dweller is probably more likely to opt for something romantic, that is natural looking but with a distinctive order and a carefully devised planting plan. Gardeners who like to propagate bedding plants will want to design a spectacular summer show every year; alpine

▶ Where water is scarce and summers are long and hot, a selection of dry-region plants makes the most effective display. The succulent plants are natives of the arid areas of Central America and Africa. The substantial proportion of evergreen species ensures a fresh look all through the year.

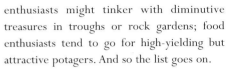

◄ Traditional 'English' style planting appears informal but depends on careful arrangement of shapes and colours. Here, the background hedge lends a note of formality to the design, but the wide variety of shrubs and perennials has been mixed to create a rich blend of hues and textures.

enthusiasts might tinker with diminutive treasures in troughs or rock gardens; food enthusiasts tend to go for high-yielding but attractive potagers. And so the list goes on.

When pondering on which style to adopt, however, it is necessary to consider which one would best suit the site, in addition to your personal preferences. A group of overhanging trees, for example, will create dappled shade that makes a successful formal flower bed almost impossible yet begs for a wild woodland planting. A small, walled, rectangular town plot is unlikely to make a happy base for a grass meadow, but could be fine for a cottage or carefully reconstructed formal garden.

It is seldom necessary, or even desirable, to keep to one particular style. Indeed, most gardens provide opportunities for several schemes, and it is the possibility of developing different projects in different parts that makes a garden interesting. Within a single space, however, particularly a small one, it is important to try to be faithful to a specific style.

Besides the relatively extensive areas shown on pages 52–131, every garden has smaller, often more problematic sites. These may be nooks and corners, crevices in walls or the footings of buildings, or simply functional barriers erected to disguise service areas, potting sheds or whatever. Every one of these presents a small but unique planting opportunity, be it a patch of wild cyclamen in the shade of a garage wall or a miniature trough set up for alpines in a dark courtyard. Limited in scope though they are, problematic though they may be, if well planted these little areas can give a garden that extra finish, transforming it from good to great. And as for style, it is possible to develop whatever individual style you fancy for these sites, or to incorporate them into a larger, overall style.

At their simplest, planting styles fall into two main categories: ordered, according to a pattern (pages 24–25), and random, which is far more *laissez-faire* (pages 26–27).

Ordered style

Ordered planting is not to be confused with formal gardening. Indeed, an ordered planting style may be informal or even naturalistic, but anything approaching a true wild, natural habitat can be developed only with random planting (pages 26–27).

In Japanese and Chinese gardens, plants are ordered to such an extent that not only is placement carefully prescribed, but the way in which each plant grows in its allotted space is also strictly controlled. In such gardens, elements of natural landscape are reconstructed in symbolic forms, creating an entire language structure that is based on philosophy and religion. Immense care is taken with positioning not only plants but also rocks, water, artefacts and pathways so that the opposing elements of *yin* and *yang* (female and male, or, if you like, hot and cool) are balanced. And yet, the sense of nature is seldom more real than in a classic East-Asian garden.

In Western style gardens, ordered planting is found in formal bedding schemes, and in such semi-formal projects as the ornamental kitchen garden shown on pages 76–81.

In so many of the Western world's suburban front gardens, routine practice is to plant out bedding each spring to carry maximum colour throughout the summer. From Alaska to Zurich, beds of French or African marigolds, red geraniums, blue lobelia and petunias or busy Lizzies of all colours are commonplace. At their simplest, such beds are a crude painting of bold colours, designed to cheer up the street; at their most sophisticated, colours of flowers and foliage textures are cunningly combined to create symmetrical but fascinating patterns of vegetation, which soften hard edges and bring a site to life.

A kitchen garden has to be ordered if it is to function effectively. This is a busy zone, where subtractions and additions are going on throughout the growing season, and where easy access is essential at all times. The most productive kitchen gardens will not look beautiful at all times: Brussels sprout plants or purple sprouting broccoli that are more than half-way harvested look gaunt and horrible at winter's end, and ugly gaps are left in the planting pattern where short-term summer crops are extracted. But in an ornamental potager such ugliness is reduced by compromising yield for appearance: a high proportion of decorative non-food plants beautify the garden but reduce its productivity.

Despite their informal appearance, classic English-style borders, as originally developed by such early twentieth-century artists as Gertrude Jekyll, are very strictly ordered. Colours, textures and shapes are rigidly co-ordinated within a pattern that may seem relaxed, but where a single plant out of place would throw the whole arrangement off balance. Some of the most revered modern-day designers seem unable to deviate from this Edwardian style, even in the face of changing times and altered values, and have merely derived their planting from those early schemes, thus perpetuating the style.

► An immaculate kitchen garden blends utility with beauty. Regimented hedges, neat alleys and strictly regulated beds help to create a fully formal effect that is pleasing to the eye, whereas the dimensions help to ensure optimum space for a succession of edible crops.

► Though informal, this border has been arranged strictly according to plant size and colour. Tall, pale-flowered plants such as the rose and *Crambe cordifolia* have been placed at measured intervals along the border back, while in the foreground a pink and blue colour theme has been replicated.

The random effect

Random placing, where plants are almost allowed to decide for themselves where they will grow, is a little more difficult to prescribe than ordered planting (pages 24–25), and takes longer to develop, but the ultimate results look much more natural. Since random planting permits much more natural growth patterns and a certain amount of self-seeding, it is often kinder to the ecology than formal gardening. The result is less tidy but more in tune with natural habitats, and therefore more welcoming to wild species, both of plants and of animals. Though it may seem at odds with today's high-tech culture, this naturalistic style is beginning to push aside some of the more contrived and rather passionless quasi-naturalistic plantings developed early this century and slavishly adhered to by so many conventional designers. In comparison with the new wild gardens, those early twentieth-century gardens are too labour intensive and too environmentally hostile.

It is almost impossible to reconstruct a truly natural habitat, of course, and so one has

▲ A random style allows the plants to grow almost where they will, but an element of control ensures optimum colour combinations. Here, pink-flowered chives (*Allium schoenoprasum*) mingle freely with blue columbines (*Aquilegia*). Both will self-seed. The oriental poppy (*Papaver orientale*) makes an exciting early summer splash – a short-lived but dramatic star turn.

► Woodland plants should be given as much freedom as possible, but it is important to arrange prominent specimens so that their foliage, flower or other characteristics are maximized. The creamy stripes of the yellow iris in the foreground, for example, make a lovely contrast with the ferns. Yellow primulas and Solomon's seal (*Polygonatum* x *hybridum*) add flower colour in this long-lasting display.

to cheat. The random effect has to be created, at first by careful placement of plants, but ultimately, in a truly naturalistic planting, plant democracy rules, as can be seen in A Dry Gravel Garden (pages 116–119), and the gardener is there merely to supervise fair play and to repel such undesirable aliens as perennial weeds or hyper-invasive plants.

Random styles include wild meadows or grass gardens, where flowering plants are encouraged to thrive in a natural sward. Here, management is very different from the normal tending of a border, with exposed soil between the plants. The grass needs to be cut back when minimal damage is done to the plants, preferably after the majority has set seed. Woodland gardens, such as A Woodland Scene (pages 112–115), are also fairly random in their planting, as are some water gardens.

Cottage gardens also depend on a certain amount of random plant development, even though they make a half-way point between cultivation and wild habitat development. They are a romantic concept (in reality, cottagers would have populated their gardens with chickens, cabbages and a pig) but the effect is of a glorious flowery muddle, kept in control, just, by laying pathways or some kind of edging round the borders. Although placing has been for specific effects such as good colour combinations, the plants are behaving as if wild, enhancing or improving on a wild habitat rather than imitating one. Spring Palette (pages 108–111) is a fine example of cottage style, where growth is natural but colour is strictly controlled.

▼ Supported by bright yellow achilleas and other foliage plants, rose campion (*Lychnis coronaria*), grasses and a mixture of hardy salvias make up the bulk of a seemingly random mix of perennials. The plants have been allowed to spread until they merge, but colour selection has been strictly controlled to ensure the desired effect is achieved.

PLANTING COMPOSITION

Wonderful and fascinating though plants are, they do not make a garden by themselves. Rather, they are the materials which a gardener uses in certain combinations and arrangements, just as other artists might use paints, words or musical notes to create a work of art. When planting a garden, therefore, it is important to understand exactly how each plant or plant group can be used to develop the whole picture. Some plants make a firm structure, others soften and blend; some are valuable for one quality, while others contribute a combination of several features.

▼ A formal framework of hedges, planted in geometric patterns, and precisely placed trees present a permanent picture. Change is effected here by using short-term bedding, which is replanted at least twice a year and set densely enough to provide a richly coloured surface.

◄ Though it is far too early for vegetables to be ready for harvesting, the ordered structure of this potager gives it permanent beauty, highlighted here by the blossoming of the cordon apples. Crops will come and go throughout the growing season, but the formal layout remains in place.

Formal framework

◄ Although it is regimented in style, this formal herb garden contains an interesting range of foliage colours, shapes and textures. Lavenders form silvery domes below clipped bay trees, while all are protected by tall cypresses which make a dark backdrop.

To succeed, to ensure a constant run of interest through the growing season, and to provide, at the very least, a pleasant overview in winter, a planting scheme must have structure. Formal planting uses symmetry and geometry, usually extending the architecture of a building or garden structure into the planting itself. Every specimen, from humble bedding to the main outline trees and shrubs, must be planted in exactly the correct spot, measured to the nearest centimetre, so that spacing is correct, not only in relation to other structures, but also in relation to each other. There is no scope for deviation from the design, here, since any single object out of true will look as awkward as a picture that does not hang straight.

Formal hedges are almost like structures themselves, often extending from walls or buildings, either creating enclosures or at least forming dividing lines. They are clipped in symmetrical outlines, rather than left to grow naturally, perhaps with fancy shapes along them, or even with topiarized sculptures.

Within a strictly formal setting, planting is measured and patterned. Some plants may be specially trained as cordons, perhaps, or as standards, that is with long, naked stems,

topped with rounded growths. The paths or border edges may be lined with clipped, ankle-height hedging, or with rows of small edging plants set symmetrically to create a clear demarcation. All this might sound fussy and unnatural, but because living plants have a wonderful ability to bring a sense of life and freshness, a formal garden can be as restful, as pleasant to stroll through and as interesting as the wildest of landscapes.

Examples of formal plantings might include any of the following: a rose garden where neat and fragrant lavender hedges offset the summer glory of the roses, and where lower, simpler plants furnish the ground between the roses; a tiny herb garden designed for a restricted space and set out in a pattern of 60cm (2ft) squares alternating with paving slabs, or arranged as triangular beds in a radial pattern, like a sliced cake; a courtyard brought to life with a series of containers, each replicated with the same collection of plants, without the architectural beauty of the place being diluted. Variations on a Potager (pages 76–81) illustrates the perfect combination of use and ornament within a formal context: a symmetrical pattern interplanted with a rich miscellany of flowers, fruit and vegetables.

Developing informality

Informal planting may appear to be random and undisciplined, but in fact structure is as important here as in the most classic of formal designs. The principles are the same: an outline of trees and shrubs must be planted to develop a firm and permanent framework. These will be as solid and dominant in their profile as a formal hedge or even a man-made structure, but must reflect a natural, rather than a contrived picture. Informal and relaxed though they are, their arrangement must be aesthetically pleasing, with varying shapes placed together to make variety, and always leading a casual eye upwards, from low and mid-height shrubs to a climactic high point.

All the foregoing presumes a planting scheme developed on empty ground, but in the majority of cases, a renewed or revised planting will take place in an existing garden where an outline of sorts is already in place. It depends what is already on the site, of course, but the chances are that it will be easier to develop an informal planting rather than a formal one, particularly if you are making major changes. A dominant tree, for instance, may have been placed as a specimen in a lawn. You may decide to install a new border round this, making the tree the central feature. Perhaps you have decided to cut an entrance through a boundary or barrier. I remember once seeing a narrow gap sliced through a huge evergreen hedge to give access to what had formerly been a hard tennis court but which had been redeveloped into an informal garden of conifers and dwarf evergreen shrubs. The hedge had originally been planted to hide the ugly caging around the tennis court and to provide protection from the wind, but in its new role it concealed the reclaimed area from the rest of the garden until, slipping through

the gap, one was rewarded with the delight of discovering a secret garden within. A wide entrance cut through the trees would have spoilt the surprise.

In informal plantings, infill, or understorey, (pages 36–39) can be wholly naturalistic, or it can follow a pattern of colours and shapes, but without resorting to geometry. In wild gardens there is minimal control beyond a casual policing of the plants to ensure fair play. In more contrived informal plantings, the composition needs to be developed with much more care. Shapes, textures and colours of plants are blended together to create the desired effect. Examples appear in the main planting recipes featured on pages 52–131, and in the smaller plant combinations dotted through the remainder of the book.

▼ Plants such as these bold pampas grasses (*Cortaderia selloana*) are useful for developing an informal display. Their grace and movement contribute to the relaxed feel of the planting, and their size enables them to dominate the scene, but without masking the other plants. The almost as large macleayas in the background are also informal in their habit.

▶ Some of the structure in this well-planted informal garden is provided by clipped hedges and the building in the background, but the bulk of the outline comes from skilfully placed trees and shrubs, with a rich infill of perennials. Though wholly informal, colours have been carefully selected, to develop a cool blue and white theme.

Combining formal with informal

▲ The neatly clipped, circular double hedge makes this design unmistakably formal, but the planting, largely of white argyranthemums and silver-leaved *Helichrysum petiolare*, has been allowed to spread in a very informal manner.

In the majority of gardens, elements of both formal and informal planting are combined. The so-called classic English style, which has been exported almost everywhere in the world, combines fairly rigid formal layouts with more relaxed planting within their boundaries. The formality carries influences from earlier styles – fragments of the parterres and knots of the sixteenth and seventeenth centuries, if you like – but within the confines of clipped hedges and boundaries, colours and shapes are allowed to tumble into each other to create a carefree summer climax. Behind immaculately clipped yew hedging, for example, big floppy shrub roses can throw out arching stems, dotted with flowers along their entire length. Among these shrubs, perennials might pick up the colours, or provide contrasting hues. Or clematis might twine randomly with the roses, but on a strictly formal pergola.

A small formal statement can often be used to bind an otherwise loose design. A cottage garden, for example, full of jumbled colours and shapes, might benefit from a formal container placed in its midst, or it could have a pair or a group of containers, all planted in exactly the same way, positioned at equal distances from each other. The formal device could be as simple as a neatly clipped hedge which lines the pathway up to the front door, separating riotous planting on one side from the ordered paving on the other. In my own garden, where planting is generally so wild as to be untidy and undisciplined, occasional formal shapes lend a little reason to the apparent irrationality of the landscapes. A row of tall, narrow junipers lines my driveway; at the edge of our terrace, one small square bed, formally replanted every autumn and spring, presents a tiny salute to a style so loved in nineteenth-century England – before designers like William Robinson and Gertrude Jekyll revolutionized the scene with their own concept of naturalistic planting – and so neglected today.

◄ A straight, paved central path and hedges clipped into cube-shaped edifices are features in this formal garden layout. Purple *Verbena bonariensis* and low-growing yellow corn marigolds have been allowed to sprawl over the pathway, softening the severity of the design and greatly enhancing the charm of the summer display.

▼ Golden privet, hostas, ferns, golden meadowsweet, ligularia, golden sedge and golden balm.

A variegated golden mix-up

The golden rule in planting is never to over-egg the pudding, and yet this lively recipe, with almost every plant present in an abnormal golden or blotched form, seems to work. A formally clipped golden privet (*Ligustrum ovalifolium* 'Aureum') is the key plant, surrounded by a jumble of plants including *Hosta* 'Francee', yellow-flowered *Ligularia przewalskii*, golden meadowsweet (*Filipendula ulmaria* 'Aurea') and the fragrant white blooms of dame's violet (*Hesperis matronalis*). In the background there are more plants with similar colouring.

Plants' special needs

This is an excellent composition for dappled shade. Such a mix would tend to scorch in strong sunlight, and might also look somewhat bilious. Most of the plants are moisture-lovers, so in dry climates apply a thick mulch in late winter, before the soil has begun to dry.

Others to try

Just look for anything with a variety name like 'Aurea' or any plant with the word 'golden' in its colloquial name.

Off-season echoes

Spring can be gorgeous with euphorbias, particularly *E. polychroma*, and with a small relative of the parsnip, *Hacquetia epipactis*.

► Mixed borders flank a paved path in a traditional country garden. The planting is largely informal, with shrubs such as variegated *Weigela florida* and deep, wine-red cottage paeonies, but the shrub in the foreground has been clipped to form a neat dome, bringing a note of formality to the border. In winter, this plant will become the focal point.

Plants as focal points

Summer glory with flowery spires

▶ Foxgloves, foxtail lilies and mulleins.

The big pink foxtail lily (*Eremurus robustus*) makes a gorgeous companion to the pink, white and purple spires of common foxgloves (*Digitalis purpurea*). Surprisingly, in such a scheme, the strident yellow mullein (*Verbascum olympicum*) makes a stately partner, not only by reason of its flowers, but also because of its huge, felty grey leaves. In the background, a broad drift of ox-eye daisies (*Leucanthemum vulgare*) completes the scene.

Plants' special needs

This is a surprising mix, because although foxgloves prefer gentle shade, they are thriving in this well-lit position, whereas eremurus and mulleins must have full sun. The soil has been enriched and mulched to enable such a flourishing mixture to grow well.

Others to try

Verbascum bombyciferum, an even more dramatic mullein, might heighten the drama further since it has larger, whiter leaves and even taller flower spikes, furnished with vivid yellow blooms. If the site proves too dry for *Digitalis purpurea*, alternative foxgloves might be the rusty orange-coloured *D. ferruginea* or the lower-growing *D. lanata*, both of which thrive in hotter, more arid conditions.

Off-season echoes

Spring bulbs would do well here, especially wild tulip species, anemones such as the scarlet *A. × fulgens* and white stars of Bethlehem (*Ornithogalum*).

Every garden, whatever the design or style, will contain some focal points. These might be constructed architectural items, such as steps, arches, gazebos or pergolas. Or, if you are fortunate enough, they could be naturally occurring features like streams, ponds, rocky outcrops or even well appointed banks. But plants make focal points, too, often more prominent than man-made features and almost always more alluring. Focal plants can be permanent, like the artistically sculpted holly tree featured in the Romantic Country Retreat (pages 72–75), or they might be relatively short-term, like a border full of vividly coloured annuals.

Show-stopping plants are usually temporary, selected to give a special fillip, but while they are performing every one of them makes a strong focal point, pulling attention from the general view to itself. A bunch of scarlet-red poppies in the middle of a mixed border, a huge and fragrant lily in a quiet, off-season shrubbery, or even the crab apple *Malus* 'John Downie' in autumn, when it is covered in crimson and yellow fruits, are all examples of horticultural 'show-stoppers'.

These glories are ephemeral, however, and too temporary to have lasting value. In most plantings, especially those that are in frequent or constant view, a more permanent focal point is needed. As the natural tendency in all of us is to focus our gaze downwards or straight ahead, such a focal point should, once it has grabbed our attention, encourage us to turn our gaze upwards. An arch, or a series of arches, will achieve this, especially if they are richly furnished with climbing plants, as in Hanging Gardens (pages 102–103). In that planting recipe, the plants shown in bloom are clematis, but in a similar situation you could select, say, *Forsythia suspensa* for early spring, a hip-bearing rambling rose for summer and autumn, and perhaps even a winter jasmine to provide bright yellow blooms on the shortest days of the year.

◄ The bright foliage of *Robinia pseudoacacia* 'Frisia' makes a strong focal point from late spring until leaf fall in autumn. Here, in late spring, a group of tall, pale foxgloves manages temporarily to snatch the limelight.

▼ Each flowering plant in this border makes a focal point. The red canna is most dominant, but the blue of the agapanthus calls for extra attention, especially as it contrasts so strongly with the red.

Filling in the understorey

The more general layer which fills in the spaces beneath the trees can be referred to as infill or understorey. In a garden, this is the chief powerhouse of artistic energy, where the scope for creative manipulation is definitely at its broadest. Rather than providing distinctive shapes for the structure, this is the part of the planting that imparts much of the essential character. Textures can be played with here, as well as colours and leaf forms. Colours can be spread brashly, or they can be stippled or dotted; discipline can be imposed with spacings and numbers, or anarchy can reign, with plants being left to do what they like.

For some, the understorey may simply consist of ground-covering plants only, grown to keep the place tidy and weed free, and as long as they stay green and healthy, without invading forbidden territory, they can be neglected. This need not look unattractive, but for even the laziest of gardeners, a well thought-out, carefully mixed ground cover will work far better than simply massing one species.

In semi-shade, under a few trees perhaps, a simple carpet of *Geranium macrorrhizum* would be pleasant almost all year long, bearing pink blossom in late spring and apple-scented foliage all summer, and turning a rust colour in autumn. But how much more attractive it would be if dotted with some white narcissus for early colour. And why not add colchicums for autumn bloom? A tall fern or two would provide relief from the monotony of the mid-summer foliage, while a clump of *Polygonatum multiflorum* would introduce interesting leaf contrast. None of these plants needs much attention after planting, and yet they will reward you year after year with variety and interest. If you wanted to, you could play with the *G. macrorrhizum* itself. There are several interesting forms, including 'Bevan's Variety' which has more shocking-pink flowers than the common form, and a near white-flowered cultivar 'Album'. *G.* × *cantabrigiense* 'Biokovo' is a gorgeous natural hybrid, discovered in the Biokov Mountains, which has inherited its

► A spacious setting with mature trees and shrubs includes a flowering dogwood (*Cornus florida*) in full bloom. The understorey planting is in cool colours: foamy white tiarella interspersed with drifts of bright blue *Phlox stolonifera*, picking up some of the colour characterisitics of a cascading stream. Later, the colours will disappear to leave a thick green carpet of foliage.

◄ French lavender, flowering sage, fragrant pinks and small, horned violas (*Viola cornuta*) lend a Mediterranean flavour to this dry garden. Additional colour comes from thyme, dwarf spiraea and an ornamental deadnettle – all plants with abundant foliage, but all relatively drought tolerant, thus providing a lush infill, even when drought threatens.

▼ Even though summer has ended and few flowers remain, leafy infill plants help to sustain a soft, living mantle in this border. The dark leaves of *Ligularia dentata* and the variegated dwarf bamboo (*Pleioblastus auricomus*) make leafy focal points among the fading foliage, but a more obvious highlight is the clump of colchicums at the foot of the foreground tree.

Hostas: understorey beauty

▼

sweet apple aroma from one parent, but a smaller, more compact habit from the other one, *G. dalmaticum*.

In the understorey just described, the plants could be allowed to develop without much restraint, but in a more formal setting, the understorey needs to be carefully measured out. At its most formal, it might consist of a bedding scheme where plants of the same kind – or in no more than two or three varieties – are spaced out at measured, regular intervals so that they develop a pattern of colour. Still formal, but a little more natural, might be a border where a loose planting plan is replicated, or partly replicated along its length. In this, a single outline, or a small outline group – an evergreen perhaps, or a standard rose or fuchsia – might form the basis for the replications, with a recurring pattern around it.

Nearly all the plants in a traditional herbaceous border are classed as understorey. That is why such borders always look better with a solid anchor, such as a tall back hedge or wall, or perhaps hedged divisions, to give the ▶

Blue-green: H. 'Halcyon', H. sieboldiana

Green: H. 'Honeybells', H. undulata

Lime and dark green: H. fortunei var. albopicta

Cream-edged: H. undulata albomarginata (syn. H. 'Thomas Hogg')

Cream in middle of leaf: H. 'Great Expectations'

Tallest: H. 'Tall Boy'

Tiniest: H. 'Gold Edger', H. venusta

Very big, pale leaves: H. 'Snowdens', H. 'Sum and Substance'

Cranesbills: natural perennials

▼

Geranium 'Anne Folkard'

G. × cantabrigiensis 'Biokovo'

G. clarkei 'Kashmir White'

G. macrorrhizum

G. × magnificum

G. pratense

G. × riversleaianum 'Russell Prichard'

G. robertianum 'Album'

G. sanguineum var. striatum

G. wallichianum 'Buxton's Variety'

planting some substance. Truly traditional herbaceous borders were dull as ditch water from late autumn, when all the plants were routinely hacked back almost to ground level, until late spring, when the first of the perennials began to bloom. Furthermore, most of the plants needed support and so unsightly frameworks, hoops, wire or sticks had to be erected before the vegetation grew up to conceal them. In modern gardens, mixed borders give far more scope for year-round delight, and it is the understorey plants which provide most of the desired series of climaxes through the year, from spring to late autumn.

The understorey usually grows more rapidly than the framework, but surprisingly, getting everything right usually takes longer. This is something to be built up gradually, rather than trying to complete it in a single season, and as it does build up it will undergo a continuing series of changes.

Practical considerations are important when planting understorey. Although a planting can be labour-saving without resorting to a single species of ground cover, the choice needs to be made with care. Invasive varieties must be planted circumspectly, especially if less vigorous plants are growing nearby. The ground must be well-prepared with every last vestige of perennial weeds removed before the first understorey plant is introduced. This chore is essential, even if it means postponing the planting project and leaving the ground bare for an entire growing season.

► Colours harmonize but textures contrast in this skilfully planted understorey. The silver-grey leaf hue is common to both the grass (*Helictotrichon sempervirens*) and the broad, felty leaves of the *Salvia argentea*.

Most perennials are quite easy to multiply, by division, from seed or in many cases from cuttings. Spreading ground-cover plants, like the geraniums described above, needs no skill at all. Just rip out chunks and push these back into the ground a metre or so away from the parents. If you are gardening on a budget, therefore, it makes a lot of sense to reserve your funds for more expensive plants that will not reproduce easily, such as outline trees and shrubs, and the more difficult perennials.

Purchase (or scrounge) the minimum numbers of understorey plants, and be ready to act like a nurseryman for a few seasons, maximizing the rate at which they will multiply until you have all you need.

Always select the very best varieties, and only those which you personally prefer. Improved forms, recognized and rewarded by such neutral bodies as Britain's Royal Horticultural Society, are the ones to seek out, provided that they meet your personal requirements and preferences. However, you should be especially wary of new plants that are promoted in aggressive marketing schemes by commercial enterprises. These may well be presented as the last word of the gardening world, but it is better to wait and see how they turn out before investing much cash in them. Growers often recommend a plant that is easy for them to propagate, and that looks enticing in a garden centre's plant section, rather than one which will give lasting value at home.

▶ The unique brownish-purple flowers of *Verbascum* 'Helen Johnson' add interest to the base of a tree, particularly where they are close to the deep blue of hardy perennial salvias. Besides providing a fillip of extra interest, this planting softens the lines and fills an empty space with foliage and colour.

Considerations of scale

Scale plays a crucial role in every planting style, whether severely formal or wild and random. A garden must contain elements of the natural landscape, but because of restrictions of size, most of these will need to be scaled down so that they can be comfortably accommodated within the space.

Trees used as outline plants will often need to be smaller than in their natural habitat. In formal gardens they might be clipped to shape or used for topiary, but even in more natural plantings they would be pruned occasionally to keep them to the desired size.

It is also very likely that gardeners will want to grow some of the other types of plant from the natural landscape – rhododendrons, say, or trilliums, or prairie perennials like gaillardias or heleniums. When such plants are taken out of their natural context, however, and arranged in the confines of a garden, some will inevitably be out of scale.

Furthermore, since a garden is invariably populated by a mixture of species from different natural habitats, it is possible for them to be out of scale with one another. This can be exacerbated where plant breeders have developed dwarf or miniature forms, or even giant ones. Consider, for example, how out of scale a miniature rose bearing 2cm (¾in) flowers on 30cm (12in) long stems might look alongside a huge and vigorous hybrid like 'The Queen Elizabeth', which, unpruned, will exceed 2m (6ft) in height.

Associating plants that are out of scale with each other is not necessarily wrong, but you do need to take care not to spoil a planting scheme by including species or varieties that would not fit in successfully. Spring daffodils, for example, come in a range of sizes from such tiny wildlings as *Narcissus bulbocodium*, which seldom exceeds 15cm (6in) in height with flowers less than 2cm (¾in) across, to huge hybrids like 'King Alfred', which grow three times as large. While each plant is fine for a particular purpose, the two would look ridiculous grown side by side. The former is ideal for naturalizing in short turf, but for brightening up a border between large spring-flowering shrubs, the latter will show up well, whereas small species might be lost to view.

There is much more to scale than simply choosing plants that look well proportioned together. Indeed, selecting a scale appropriate to the dimensions of the site should be an early consideration. In formal gardening, for example, a great deal of modern styles have been borrowed from 'Grand Manner' landscapes of earlier times, when gardening was the sole domain of large landowners or wealthy people. Thus a knot garden, parterre or potager needs to be adapted to your own plot dimensions, which will almost invariably mean scaling down. The simplest way of doing this, of course, is to reduce the overall dimensions, but it is also possible to scale down the plants themselves. Such miniaturizing will render trees, shrubs, hedges and understorey plants in proportion to one another and small enough to fit into a confined area without overcrowding. Thus, where oaks, limes, large rhododendrons and huge shrub roses might fill the space in a grand landscape, on a miniature scale small trees or evergreens sculpted down to size, dwarf azaleas and roses which grow

▶ The impression of scale in this courtyard has been effected by placing a container in the foreground. The planting in the container is so conventionally out of scale as to have become humorous. South African pineapple lilies (*Eucomis bicolor*) are crammed in with the spiky foliage of a young century plant (*Agave americana*). Both plants grow very much taller in the wild, the century plant achieving a rosette 2m (6ft) wide before flowering.

Scale and texture

► *Verbascum chaixii* 'Album' with *Hordeum jubatum*.

An almost comical effect is achieved here by blending a relatively low-growing mullein (*Verbascum chaixii* 'Album') with squirrel tail grass (*Hordeum jubatum*). This mullein has 60cm (2ft) spikes whereas the feathery inflorescences of the grass can stand as high as 1m (3ft). The plants also make a delightful textural contrast.

Plants' special needs

Both plants do best in light or medium, free-draining soil that is reasonably fertile but not overfed. The grass can be multiplied from seedlings and although the mullein will produce seed, it can also be propagated from root cuttings or, unlike most of its tribe, by division.

Others to try

Lots of different grasses are attractive when planted together, but to repeat this strange, out-of-scale effect, a contrasting plant is needed. Some of the taller penstemons would be good, perhaps *P.* 'Alice Hindley', which is a soft blue to mauve, or a strident red as in 'King George'. Alternatively, you could try a bright orange or white red-hot poker (*Kniphofia*).

Off-season echoes

Grasses will continue to contribute long after they have died off and turned brown, but the mullein is a medium-term summer plant and could be replaced, or supported, at other seasons. *Thermopsis montana* could make a pretty spring substitute, its distinctive yellow spikes providing outline while the young grass develops. In autumn, the purple bead-like flowers of *Liriope muscari* would also make a good companion.

more modestly can achieve a roughly similar effect. A vast potager, the size of the great kitchen garden at Villandry, in France, is even easier to scale down since, instead of having hundreds of rectangular or triangular vegetable beds, each bordered with hedges and pathways, you can have two or three, or even one, and scale the bed size down to as little as a 2m (6ft) square.

In a small garden, or a small division within a garden, juggling with different scales can often produce surprising results. Sometimes, canny placing of an outsize plant, especially in a prominent spot, will alter the whole appearance of a planting, or, in the case of a short-lived perennial or biennial, will give a temporary shift to the profile. This gives a gentle jolt to the senses and thus adds extra interest and, often, extra beauty to a setting.

▲ **Giant thistles (*Onopordum nervosum*) tower to a height of 2m (6ft) or more above the grasses and wildflowers in a meadow, giving a harder, more noticeable profile. Such a plant combination might look odd in the wild, but in a garden it adds an extra dimension – height – and though the plants are out of scale, they do not detract from the natural look of the meadow.**

Spacing plants

◀ Where ground-cover plants may turn out to be dull at certain times of year, interest can be sustained by breaking the spacing rules and introducing companion plants which, in season, become focal points. Here, the South American *Tropaeolum polyphyllum* trails its glaucous leaves and vivid yellow blooms over the top of a carpet of low-growing sedum.

resulting in a dense, amorphous mess where the plants are unable to fulfil their individual shapes. If you do plant too densely – and almost everyone does – be prepared to thin ruthlessly a couple of seasons later.

Another factor to bear in mind is that although every plant has its own natural dimensions, these will vary according to local conditions. A rule of thumb that I use with shrubs is to separate them by a space equal to their expected vertical height. Thus if you expect the shrub to grow to 2m (6ft), allow at least 2m (6ft) between it and its nearest

Much sleep is lost, especially by beginner gardeners, over the correct spacing of plants. The most accurate general answer to the question of how far apart to plant, is that it probably does not really matter. It is better to use your natural instinct than to mess about with rulers, strings or any other measuring instruments. You are planting living things, rather than decorating a room or building an edifice, and since plants have a life of their own, it is hard to predict exactly how they will grow. The trick is to relax, make an attempt at getting it more or less right, and then stand back to see what happens.

The only really valid argument for recommending spacings is to provide information on ultimate spread and height of plants in an association. In the planting schemes illustrated later in this book (pages 52–131), spacings are suggested in the plant lists. These are loose recommendations, rather than figures to be strictly adhered to, designed to show the optimum spacing for plants – that is, spacings that will allow optimum growth without inhibiting neighbouring plants. If you wish to economize, it is perfectly acceptable to increase the distance between plants and reduce their numbers. The only consequence is that the scheme will take a little longer to mature. Conversely, in some cases, especially with ground-cover plants, closer spacing will speed development but may bring forward the time when you need to thin out your plants.

If you miscalculate, most errors can be rectified. The most common mistake is to underestimate the amount of space a mature plant will need. With herbaceous plants this poses little difficulty, since they tend to merge together anyway. If trees and shrubs are too closely crowded, growth will be inhibited, neighbouring shrub. This does not work for tall, thin or low, fat shrubs, of course, but it does give a very rough idea. You will be disappointed at planting, since the poor little things look so isolated, but eventually they will mature to take up the spaces. Meanwhile, you can fill the gaps with interim plants – fast-growing shrubs that provide a quick display while the other shrubs develop. Remove them as soon as they begin to inhibit the growth of the more permanent shrubs.

It is not always desirable for outline plants to stand apart. Often, especially with open-habited species, you will want their branches to merge. In this case, closer planting is perfectly acceptable. The Speedy Shrubs and Climbers planting (pages 128–131) shows how well plants can blend into each other.

There are no general rules for smaller herbaceous plants, since they all have individual growth habits. Most good reference books supply ultimate expected dimensions, and, since the aim is for the plants to merge, it makes sense to take note of these statistics and to plant so that they will merge without overcrowding. Since it is easy to thin herbaceous plants out, there is no need to be obsessive about densities. To save on expenditure, plant more sparsely, then divide and replant later.

Direct-sown annuals can thrive untended in nature. If you sow them thinly, all you need do is pull out a few seedlings where overcrowding has occurred. If I can be bothered, I usually thin out such plants as poppies, cornflowers, nigellas, eschscholzias and calendulas to about 20cm (8in) apart. All that happens if I do not thin them is that dense populations fail to produce large plants with good frames, which results in a curtailed flowering period.

◀ In formal gardening plant spacing needs to be precise, but even so, the rigid nature of a formal design will often benefit from a little licence. Here, the clipped tree in the background is severe in its neatness, but the red-flowered *Clematis* 'Royal Velours' in the foreground brings a more relaxed note, growing as it does with disregard for strict measurements.

▶ In an informal mixed border plants should be spaced to allow optimum development. It is important neither to overcrowd nor to plant too sparsely. Here, delphiniums, roses and lilies are perfectly spaced to produce a pleasing display.

CREATING WITH COLOUR

Colours speak an eloquent language, different hues stimulating different emotions or moods, and they offer the gardener more than mere brightness or contrast. Judicious, well-managed use of hue – not only in flowers, but in leaves, stems, seedheads or fruits – will result in a far more pleasing display than where plants are assembled without regard to colour harmony. This does not mean that a creative gardener needs to be restrained, or to develop a garden that lacks passion and daring. Far from it. But whatever your preferences, it cannot but help to know what colours can do for you, and how they can best be deployed to achieve the desired results.

▼ A startling contrast that works surprisingly well. The shocking-pink flowers of a Japanese azalea may clash with the orange form of the Welsh poppy (*Meconopsis cambrica*), but the combination is bright enough to draw attention to itself, and is only in evidence for a brief period in the gardening year. Hot colours work especially well in spring, when cold weather is a common threat and skies can be dull.

Using colour

Flower colour and, to almost as great an extent, foliage colour can be used to develop particular moods and styles in a garden. A single colour theme gives a stronger effect than a mix, and if that theme is in warm colours – red, yellow or orange – the result will be 'hot'. Conversely, a border in blue or white, or even green, will be 'cool'. Thus the white-variegated foliage of the grass *Holcus mollis* 'Albovariegatus' planted with blue forget-me-nots or brunneras creates an ice-cold combination whereas roses in peachy tones makes a warm blend, and a planting of orange or red poppies is even hotter. Massing plants together has the effect of intensifying flower colour, especially if the blooms are conspicuous. Looser, less dense plantings produce a more diffuse effect.

Strong, bright colours carry an instant impact. A bed of bright red geraniums or the amazing spectacle of Dutch tulip fields in full flower, for example, are impossible to miss, and

may even provoke a gasp of surprise. Softer pastel hues in gardens can have as great an impact, but elicit very different reactions. A formal rose garden, for example, all soft pinks with, perhaps, pale blue understorey plants, will create a memorable effect of peace and contentment rather than a dramatic thrill.

In any scheme, it is important to be selective about the colour range. And the more colour there is, the more selective you must be. In a largely green, naturalistic planting, like A Shady Urban Oasis (pages 94–97), flower colours play a low-key role, but green is all important. The antithesis of this is formal bedding, where flowers are used outdoors in the same way that soft furnishing fabric might be deployed indoors that is, to cover entire surfaces with specific colours and textures. You must be as rigorous in your choice of hues among your bedding plants as you would be in selecting curtain material, carpets or kitchen

▲ In a magnificently planted white border, shaggy, yellow-centred *Leucanthemum maximum* is the centrepiece, supported by white forms of rose campion (*Lychnis coronaria* Alba Group) and white musk mallow (*Malva moschata alba*). All this coolness is supported by herbaceous *Artemisia ludoviciana*, whose young foliage is such a pale shade of grey that it looks silver.

surfaces. There is an added complication, of course, because whereas colours in a room remain constant, flowers and plants in a garden undergo a series of changes. Most planting schemes fall between these two extremes, however, and planting is more likely to be varied, rather than bedded out in solid sheets, and flower and foliage will be more balanced.

It is possible to plant so that colour schemes change from one season to the next, or, conversely, the same, or nearly the same colours, can be retained through the whole year by using a succession of different plants with similar colours. A pink and white combination of roses in a formal bed, for example, can be replicated in spring with pink and white tulips. A predominantly blue summer theme of lavender and mauve perennials – cranesbills, perhaps, with polemoniums and catananche – can be extended into autumn with perennial asters such as *A. × frikartii*

'Mönch'. In spring, similar colours could be provided by *Lathyrus vernus cyaneus* and Spanish bluebells (*Hyacinthoides hispanica*), or by pulmonarias or mertensias.

Making sweeping seasonal colour changes is more dramatic, however, with hot colours to warm everyone up in spring, perhaps, followed by a cooler theme for the summer. You could do this by growing orange or red tulips – try *Tulipa* 'Prinses Irene' and 'Apeldoorn' – supported by orange pansies, bright golden doronicums or, if you dare, huge orange or yellow crown imperials (*Fritillaria imperialis*). Amazingly, such hot colours can look good with pink spring blossom on overhanging trees. In summer, lots of creams and blues or whites could be used to tone everything down. For instance, *Phlox paniculata* 'Fujiyama', white as driven snow, makes a clean contrast with the cool blue of delphiniums or with summer monkshood (*Aconitum*).

Adding some hostas with white or cream variegations, or perhaps a group of white or very pale pink astilbes, would tone down the spring fever and play it distinctly cool.

The colour schemes in many of the planting recipes illustrated in this book (pages 52–131) have been kept simple. When planting any of these recipes, there is no need to follow rigidly the colour schemes given. Most of the plants used are available in several other colours, so by selecting different varieties it should be possible to alter the hues of a recipe without undermining the central theme. If key colours are changed, it is important that the sense of harmony is not lost, or the simplicity spoilt by slipping into an indiscriminate mixture. Where one of two contrasting colours is changed – blue into pink, perhaps, or yellow into red – then the other principal colour must also be reviewed, to ensure that an equally pleasing composition remains.

Colour for harmony

In some planting schemes the dominance of a single colour provides much of the artistic strength. Single or restricted colour schemes are always more efffective than mixtures, because in the latter the different colours tend to balance one another. A bed of concentrated reds, for example, such as the Red-hot Border (pages 82–85), makes a hot-looking display that is vibrant in summer sunshine, but which

tones itself down to a sulky glow in twilight. It is the imbalance of the red border – natural looking in its plant distribution, but unlikely in a truly wild landscape – that gives it appeal.

Even in a mixed border, harmonized shades will usually work more effectively than a hotchpotch of different colours. Imagine, for instance, an area in the garden where similar tones are arrayed, oranges perhaps, with a

small divergence either way to yellows in one direction, or edging towards scarlet in the other. Even though the variation of hues is wide, they are all within a particular band on the colour spectrum, and therefore achieve a harmonious effect.

A more specific example of this would be a small border planted around the apricot-coloured rose, *Rosa* 'Buff Beauty'. It might

► The colour of pale or albino flowers varies in quality from pure white, as seen in these double daisies, to the softer, creamy tones of the tulips. The cream-marked hosta helps to accentuate the purity of the white flowers, while harmonizing with the silvery artemisia leaves and making a handsome foil for the stark white, tiny-flowered forget-me-nots.

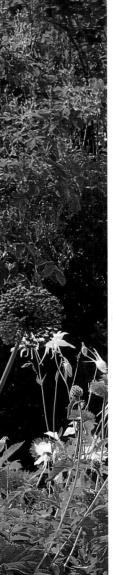

◄ In a sombrely coloured midsummer scheme, rounded purple heads of *Allium hollandicum* 'Purple Sensation' make a textural contrast with purple and cream, spire-shaped lupins and similarly tall foxgloves in the background. Old roses and centaureas introduce a pink tendency, with a white flower or two from some of the foxgloves creating a highlight.

contain some foxgloves – *Digitalis purpurea* 'Sutton's Apricot' for early summer, followed by the rust-coloured *D. ferruginea*. Low-growing plants could include the joyful pansy 'Jolly Joker', whose large flowers combine warm orange with purple-blue, and perhaps the coppery-salmon pea flowers of *Lathyrus vernus*. In spring, before the rose blooms, similarly coloured plants could give a prelude of what is to follow. The gorgeous tan and orange tulip, *Tulipa* 'Prinses Irene', for instance, would look lovely against the liverish-bronze of the emerging rose foliage. The variety of plants in this border ensures that interest never fades, yet the colour theme is adhered to, creating a calming sense of order.

Similar harmonies can be built around almost any colour you choose. White gardens, red borders or yellow planting designs all make potential colour schemes with almost unlimited choices. Purples are wonderful for sultry summer displays, with heliotropes, centaureas, echinaceas, liatris and a whole range of perennials. Purple, a combinaton of the primary colours red and blue, bridges the gap between warm and cool hues. It can be sombre, toning down hot or vibrant colours, but it can also be intense and bright, bringing life to a pale scheme.

Red leaves, red fruits

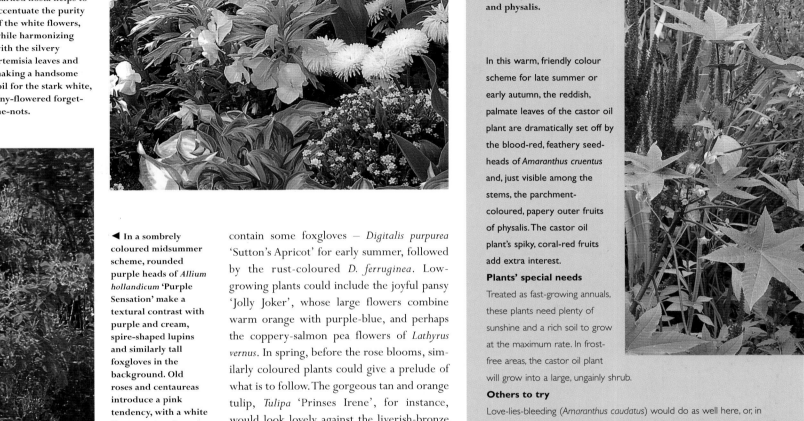

► Castor oil plant (*Ricinus communis*) with prince's feather (*Amaranthus cruentus*) and physalis.

In this warm, friendly colour scheme for late summer or early autumn, the reddish, palmate leaves of the castor oil plant are dramatically set off by the blood-red, feathery seed-heads of *Amaranthus cruentus* and, just visible among the stems, the parchment-coloured, papery outer fruits of physalis. The castor oil plant's spiky, coral-red fruits add extra interest.

Plants' special needs
Treated as fast-growing annuals, these plants need plenty of sunshine and a rich soil to grow at the maximum rate. In frost-free areas, the castor oil plant will grow into a large, ungainly shrub.

Others to try
Love-lies-bleeding (*Amaranthus caudatus*) would do as well here, or, in moist soil, try *Rheum palmatum*, for both foliage and flower effect.

Off-season echoes
Spring foliage of paeonies can be a rich coppery red and looks wonderful with tulips, or with blood-red wallflowers.

Such strict colour schemes are by no means the only way. Indeed, you might abhor the artificiality of such a manipulated planting design, but it will always be rewarding to experiment with solo colour arrangements, partly because they enable you to learn so much about how colour functions in a garden, but mainly because when they succeed, they create memorable displays.

Contrast for effect

◀ The rat-tail dock (*Persicaria amplexicaulis* 'Firetail') carries vivid red blooms above ever-green foliage, making a striking contrast with the midnight-purple *Phlox paniculata* 'Le Mahdi'.

▶ The late-blooming *Clematis* 'Jackmanii Superba' presents its large, satin-textured, purple flowers among the golden-yellow leaves of the European elder (*Sambucus racemosa* 'Aurea'). Growing climbers through host plants is an effective way of developing perfect associations.

Purple plants for contrast

▼

Strong colour contrasts can be even more beautiful than those created by simple colour harmonies (pages 46–47), and some combinations are so effective that they have become classics: red with yellow or with green, black with gold, pink with pale lemon, and tan with navy blue.

Strongly contrasting colours neutralize one another, creating a completely different effect from that of a single-colour theme border. Sharp yellow, for example, makes a rich contrast with deep blue: try planting *Anchusa azurea* 'Loddon Royalist' with yellow verbascums or a yellow lily, or growing yellow dwarf tulips with blue polyanthus or grape hyacinths (*Muscari*), or cornflowers with buttercups. Purple and gold make a wonderful combination. Salmon or apricot with deep maroon-red is more subtle: try apricot *Rosa* 'Lady Hillingdon' with the red *Clematis* 'Madame Julia Correvon' for a great summer blend. The less obvious colour combination of bright red and emerald green – perhaps more memorably associated with parrots than with flowers – is never more gloriously evident than when the black and green widow iris (*Hermodactylus tuberosus*) is grown with the vivid scarlet *Anemone × fulgens*. Both these colours occur together in the flowers of the extremely beautiful South American lily *Alstroemeria psittacina* (syn. *A. pulchella*).

A contrast can be gentle, too, particularly when flower and foliage are composed together so as to create specific effects. Silver foliage shows up starkly against strong reds or oranges, for instance, but makes a far more subtle contrast with white or pale pink. Thus, the silver foliage of, say, *Artemisia ludoviciana* is as effective when used as part of a white garden, where it has a warming effect, as it would when used for toning down such strong hot colours as red poppies or penstemons. This actual effect is easy to see on the same plant if you compare red and white carnations, both of which have silver foliage.

Aubrietas, purple and rosy-mauve shades to enliven spring rock gardens or walls

Erysimum **'Bowles Mauve'**, for gentle contrast with yellow spring flowers

Heliotropium arborescens **'Cherry Pie'**, deep purple to tone down the brightness of orange gazanias

Lathyrus vernus, rose-purple to contrast with pale yellow primulas or to harmonize with purple honesty (*Lunaria annua*)

Rosa **'Zéphirine Drouhin'**, creates a wine-coloured theme with dark purple *Penstemon* **'Burgundy'**

Salvia officinalis **Purpurascens Group**, warms up silvery foliage themes

Tulipa **'Maytime'**, **'Negrita'** or **'Queen of Night'**, perfect with ivory wallflowers or soft golds and yellow

▲ Contrasting or complementary colours within a single flower are especially valuable in small, detailed plantings. Here, the pansy 'Jolly Joker' shows a classic combination – orange with purple – which, with the supporting freshness of the surrounding foliage, makes a delightful cameo display. The bronzing flowers of the closely planted *Euphorbia cyparissias* reflect the warm tones of the pansies.

◀ The warm ochre and dusky-yellow petals of the early flowering hybrid lily (*Lilium* 'Festival') make a strong contrast with the peacock-blue flowers of *Anchusa azurea* 'Loddon Royalist'.

Working with background colour

As foliage makes up the bulk of any planting, rather than flower, it is a major factor in decision-making about colour. And all the subtle colour suffusions of the foliage must be made to echo the stronger themes of the flowers.

In nature, foliage usually does match flower colour well, and in a garden this can be enhanced by the thoughtful selection of plants that have particular foliage attributes, not merely in colour but also in texture and shape. Shrubs or trees with purple or bronze foliage, for example, support strong reds, as can be seen in A Bronze Border (pages 124–127), but also look very good with coppery tones. Newly developing shoots on the universally popular rose *Rosa* 'Albertine', for example, are deep purple, making a dark foil for its salmon flowers.

An often repeated and delightful plant combination is the golden-leaved hop (*Humulus lupulus* 'Aureus') intertwined with the midnight blue-flowered clematis, *C.* 'Etoile Violette'. This flowers in summer, after the longest day, but to replicate that lime-green and blue duet earlier in the year, try growing the spring-flowering *C. alpina* 'Frances Rivis' with the green and gold ivy *Hedera colchica* 'Sulphur Heart'.

Besides interacting with each other, plant colours must sit comfortably with their surroundings. Man-made structures such as walls, fences and other garden features can assert a major influence in the choice of a particular colour scheme. If flower colours shout at building fabric, or at surrounding paintwork, one or other must be changed, and it is usually cheaper and easier to replant than to rebuild. (I still shudder at the memory of a livid pink cherry variety, *Prunus jamasakura* 'Kanzan', in full blossom up against the hot, red brickwork of a newly built house.) Sometimes all that is needed is a minor shift in hue, no more than a tone or so in pink, say from salmon to rose, or from pale, pure blue to darker, more purplish tint.

When associating flowers with surrounding materials, it is often hard to blend like colours with like. With red or reddish brickwork, for example, flowers in shades of red and pink can look out of kilter, whereas creams, soft yellows and rich purples can work well. Greyish or buff limestone, or even cold, grey granite make a superb background for the soft, smoky blue of *Wisteria sinensis* and for the richer purple of *Clematis* 'Jackmanii Superba'.

▶ One of the finest purple-leaved shrubs in cultivation is a form of Canadian Judas Tree, (*Cercis canadensis* 'Forest Pansy'). Here, the rich hue of its leaves – like a full-bodied red wine – makes a dark but pleasing background to the emerging sprays of *Crambe cordifolia*.

◀ A high wall, painted terracotta, makes a warm, bright background to a small herb garden planted with golden marjoram and chives. The effect of the wall is softened, however, by planting fremontodendrons, white *Abutilon vitifolium* and other wall plants against it.

Graceful form with luscious colours

◄ *Clematis* 'Etoile Rose' with smokebush foliage and cranesbill flowers.

The elegant, curled blooms of summer-flowering *Clematis* 'Etoile Rose' are a unique shade of cerise-pink, each with a paler line along the edges of the satin-like sepals. The colour, and the shapes of these blooms, make a beautiful contrast with the blue-mauve cranesbill (*Geranium* 'Johnson's Blue') and the dark purple foliage of *Cotinus coggygria* 'Royal Purple' as a background.

Plants' special needs

Happy on any reasonable soil, these plants will work well together in sun or in semi-shade. Cool roots are essential for clematis – shaded here by the smoke-bush – and, since this and the cranesbill both need to be cut back before the growing season begins, a gentle spring feed of general fertilizer is recommended.

Others to try

In some areas, *Clematis* 'Etoile Rose' can be difficult to establish. A robust alternative is *C.* 'Minuet' whose flowers are purplish-pink, with paler centres to the sepals. A good cranesbill alternative would be *Geranium clarkei* 'Kashmir Purple', or you could plant a purple or blue penstemon. Try *P.* 'Sour Grapes' or 'Stapleford Gem.'

Off-season echoes

No spring blossom has quite the colour or texture of *Clematis* 'Etoile Rose' but spring-blooming *C. alpina* 'Ruby' might provide a similar effect. The early blooming rose, *Rosa* 'Pompon de Paris' is covered with small, double pink blooms and looks beautiful with early blue or purple flowers such as *Hyacinthoides hispanica* (syn. *Scilla hispanica*) or *Lathyrus vernus*. For autumn, consider the glorious red *Tropaeolum speciosum*.

◄ Warm, glowing flower colour, seen here in an orange form of yarrow (*Achillea millefolium*), is made even warmer by its background of golden and variegated foliage. Assembling shrubs with coloured foliage requires skill: too many variables results in a fussy, restless picture, but these plants make a simple but near-perfect display.

There is no substitute for subjecting a real garden to scrutiny and analyzing how and why its planting works. This section of the book takes you as close as possible to that experience. We look in detail at 20 specific, yet generic, plantings, each the unique work of an accomplished gardener. Together they cover a range of planting styles as well as widely varied situations, so there should be something to appeal to all tastes and match the conditions of different garden sites.

With the aid of colour artworks showing the plan of each planting and a separate keyed-in list of plant ingredients, you can see exactly how a border, or plant group, is composed, down to the precise numbers of each species used. Each 'recipe' is fully explained and illustrated, with views of the planting and portraits of its key plants. Instructions are given on preparing the site, planting up and future maintenance. Descriptive profiles for five or six of the plants in each recipe build up across the section to a directory of over 100 plants.

If you wish to stick closely to the recipes, do so: they will all work well, since each has been drawn from a well-designed and imaginatively planted real garden. But each scheme can be used as a springboard for your own creative input, providing the seeds of a planting idea but allowing you the freedom to interpret it as you like.

▲ A succession of interest is ensured in this water garden. The green leaves of the early-flowering double campion and irises will harmonize later with the bronze foliage of the emerging rodgersias whose flowers, when fully opened, herald the summer climax.

Planting recipes

AN AROMATIC GRAVEL GARDEN

This naturalistic planting of self-seeding annuals and perennials in warm colours is backed up with a mix of evergreen foliage to ensure year-round freshness. The gritty surface helps to give the impression of an arid semi-desert that has brought forth bloom after rain, but with this plant selection, colour and greenery will hold, even during prolonged drought. Bright hues – reds, oranges and salmons – work best in strong sun, and the addition of aromatic herbs ensures rich fragrance. Off-season interest is maintained by bulbous species which pop up with surprise displays through autumn, winter and spring.

In high summer, members of the poppy family provide most of the colour in this informal scheme, supported by cranesbills with musk mallow, pink hyssop and the dark crimson *Knautia macedonica*. For outline, mulleins and foxgloves create a series of spires within the bed, which is backed by an

▲ Opium poppy (*Papaver somniferum*) is as attractive in seed, even when the capsules dry out, as in flower, when the petal colours range through deep magentas, pinks and reds to white.

old brick wall bearing a purple-leaved vine. Small hollies and low, rounded box bushes introduce permanent 'structure', but the area might gain by the addition of a container or a sculpture. Open spaces and pathways among the plants mean that the aromatic herbs, including sages, coriander, a variety of thymes and catnip (*Calamintha nepetoides*) can be enjoyed at close quarters.

Off-season interest is maintained with cyclamen and fritillaries for spring, as well as South African nerines and *Kniphofia caulescens* for autumn. The little blue violas are in bloom right through the year and are backed up by such evergreens as *Daphne collina* and sage. This is a 'pop it in' garden where you can experiment with different annuals, letting them grow as they wish. Try cooling down colours by exchanging the Californian poppies with blue larkspurs, or with pearly-hued field poppies.

▲ Californian poppy (*Eschscholzia californica*) is a sun-loving annual that is easily grown from seed.

◀ The key to success with this planting is to encourage natural propagation. Most of the plants will self-seed readily, and once the area is established the gardener's job is simply to police plant populations, thinning out to make sure that no single variety becomes too dominant. Ideal conditions would be free-draining soil, in full sun. The grit mulch is not essential, but it helps create a pleasant surface and improves growing conditions for many of the plants, especially those species that dislike damp conditions. No feeding or watering is needed, but weeding must be done with care, to preserve volunteer seedlings.

Planting Plan   3m x 6m (10ft x 20ft)

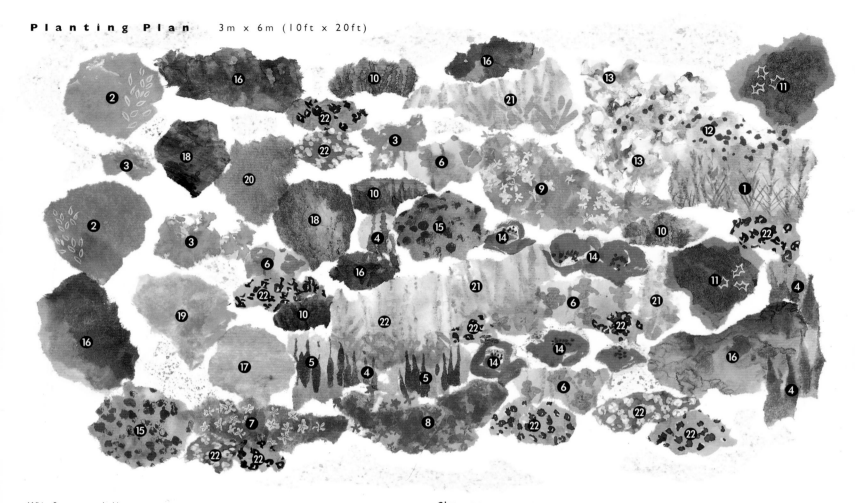

White flowers are valuable for making strong contrasts. Here, blooms of white musk mallow (*Malva moschata* f. *alba*) blend with an apricot form of Californian poppy.

❧ The tall flower spikes of this rust-coloured foxglove (*Digitalis ferruginea*) make a striking statement. Unlike the common foxglove, this species enjoys dry, sunny conditions.

The yellow flowers of *Asphodeline liburnica* open each morning to contrast with the crimson scabious (*Knautia macedonica*). By afternoon the asphodel blooms have withered, but their feathery foliage continues its display.

❧ *Papaver rhoeas* has been developed into several colour ranges for gardens. Besides the natural red, there are now field poppies in soft pinks, lemons, picotees and even pearl-grey.

❧ The simple leaves of purple sage (*Salvia officinalis* 'Purpurascens') contrast with the deeply lobed foliage of *Geranium pratense*.

❧ The pale blue flowers of *Geranium pratense* 'Mrs Kendall Clark' provide a cooling contrast to the apricot tones of the main planting.

Ingredients

Key	Plant	Qty / Space (cm)	Substitute
①	Asphodeline liburnica	>3 /45	A. luteus
②	Buxus sempervirens	2/60	Sarcococca humilis
③	Coriandrum sativum	>5 /20	Salvia horminum
④	Digitalis ferruginea	>5 /90	D. pauciflora
⑤	Digitalis purpurea	>5 /90	Penstemon
⑥	Eschscholzia californica	*	Calendula
⑦	Geranium clarkei 'Kashmir White'	3 /30	G. sylvaticum 'Album', G. renardii
⑧	Geranium himalayense	>3 /30	G. 'Johnson's Blue'
⑨	Geranium pratense 'Mrs Kendall Clark'	>5 /45	G. psilostemon, G. magnificum
⑩	Hyssopus officinalis (pink form)	>3 /90	Lavandula, Rosmarinus
⑪	Ilex aquifolium 'Hascombensis'	2/60	I. a. 'Green Pillar'
⑫	Knautia macedonica	>7 /45	Scabiosa 'Butterfly Blue'
⑬	Malva moschata f. alba	>3 /60	Gaura lindheimeri
⑭	Papaver rhoeas	*	P. somniferum, P. lateritum
⑮	Rosa 'Oakington Ruby'	2 /60	Prunus incisa 'Kojo-no-mai'
⑯	Salvia officinalis 'Purpurascens Variegata'	2 /60	S. o. 'Tricolor'
⑰	Thymus 'Anderson's Gold'	3 /45	Any golden thyme
⑱	Thymus 'Doone Valley'	I /45	Any variegated thyme
⑲	Thymus x citriodorus 'Silver Posie'	3 /30	Any thyme
⑳	Thymus serpyllum 'Pink Chintz'	3 /30	T. s. 'Russetings', T. 'Album'
㉑	Verbascum thapsus	*	V. blattaria, V. olympicum
㉒	Viola tricolor	*	Any pansies or violas

Qty: *the number of specimens used in this recipe; numbers can be adjusted to suit a different site.*
Space: *recommended spacings for optimum growth (in centimetres).*

Notes: Where no number is given, allow seedlings to develop ad lib, or plants to spread, but thin them out to avoid overcrowding.
* = start with 1 packet of seed

❧ Californian poppies, naturally orange, have been selected for paler, softer hues here. They will self-seed but can become invasive, if the majority of stems are not cut back after flowering.

❧ Mulleins (*Verbascum*) provide soft, velvet texture with their silver-grey foliage, as well as strong yellow colour with their flowers.

◄ Tall, thin foxgloves (*Digitalis ferruginea*) and wild mulleins (*Verbascum thapsus*) add an architectural element to this largely herbaceous planting.

Groundwork: Ensure that the ground is well dug, levelled and firmed, but not compacted, and is free from all perennial weeds before laying down a gravel scree. A layer of 5–7.5cm (2–3in) of 1cm (½in) gravel will suffice. When planting, scrape the gravel back first. Any soil left on the surface will wash through with rain.

Planting procedure: Hardy annuals can be sown direct – scatter seeds on the gravel and water in with a rose. Thin out young seedlings to 20cm (8in) apart for small and medium plants, 1m (3ft) apart for mulleins and foxgloves. Do not space too evenly – aim for a natural look.

Group together perennials such as knautias, asphodels and cranesbills to create zones of taller, thicker vegetation. Leave some areas of gravel bare and place small plants at the edges of these. The idea is to be able to walk easily among the plants.

Maintenance: Dead-head to reduce surplus seed and pull up weeds before they set seed. Divide perennials every few years and prune evergreen shrubs to their desired shape. Make selections of emerging annuals by pulling out undesirable colours as soon as their first flowers open. Keep building up the numbers of bulbs for off-season colour.

PLANT DIRECTORY

❧ **Digitalis**
Foxglove. The common European species, *D. purpurea*, is happiest in semi-shade where it grows to 1m (3ft) or more, bearing tubular flowers with speckled throats in purple, pink or white. More sun-loving species include the rust-coloured *Digitalis ferruginea*, which is a longer-lived perennial with narrower, glossier leaves. Propagate from seed, either self-sown, or by collecting seeds to sow in autumn.

❧ **Eschscholzia**
Californian poppy. Very vigorous annuals with feathery, blue-grey foliage and four-petalled flowers in warm, vivid colours. In the wild, the species *E. californica* has bright orange or yellow blooms, but garden selections include flowers in more gentle, peachy tones of salmon-pink or soft apricot. Copious seeders, developing large colonies of self-sown progeny in a single season. Sow direct into the ground in spring or autumn.

❧ **Geranium pratense**
Meadow cranesbills. European natives with deeply lobed basal leaves and five-petalled flowers from midsummer. Commonly deep blue, but there are white forms, double-flowered varieties such as *G. p.* 'Flore Pleno', and 'Mrs Kendall Clark' whose lavender-blue flowers bear pinkish veins.

❧ **Papaver**
Poppies. Good species for gardens include *P. opulum* and *P. rhoeas*, both European cornfield weeds, and the opium poppy (*P. somniferum*). The former have vivid red flowers – though there are selections for pink and even white forms – whereas opium poppies have handsome, glaucous foliage and flowers in a range of hues from deep purple through to pink.

❧ **Salvia officinalis**
Common sage. Useful and decorative shrubby herbs, growing to about 50cm (20in), with simple leaves which can be dried for winter use and spikes of royal-blue flowers in summer. Coloured-leaved forms such as 'Icterina' (yellow and green) and 'Purpurascens' are as pleasantly flavoured as more culinary green forms.

❧ **Verbascum**
Mulleins. The species in this planting is the northern European *V. thapsus*, but Mediterranean species such as *V. olympicum* or *V. bombyciferum* are more spectacular. In good conditions, many will exceed 2.5m (8ft) in height and are copious seeders. Most are biennial, but *V. nigrum* and *V. x phoeniceum* are perennial. Susceptible to predations from mullein moth.

IN THE SHELTER OF A SUNNY WALL

Protected from the harsh climate in the open, this warm, sunny corner has had its soil enriched to support a varied collection of plants, from drought-tolerant Mediterranean subjects to species from moister, cooler habitats. The tall limestone wall is high enough to ensure total privacy and would provide a handsome backdrop whether it faced east or west, as well as minimizing the effect of damaging winds. This is a wide border, with plenty of space for shrubs, even small trees, as well as an inspired mix of perennials, sub-shrubs and temporary summer highlight plants.

◀ Hot colours and exotic blooms for a hot position: scarlet penstemons and a pair of startling three-petalled tigridias in red and yellow make an eye-catching contrast with the brick-pink of the *Diascia rigescens*.

In this daring colour scheme the central theme is blue or purple-blue and gold, with strands running to pink, maroon and even bright scarlet. Gold or yellow comes from foliage as well as flower. Along the border edge, golden marjoram, rosemary and cotton lavender merge their fragrances as well as their leaves. The aromatic effect is intensified in hot sun, when heat from the stone pathway helps their essential oils to vaporize. Behind them, the luxuriant foliage of asters, kniphofias and fast-growing shrubs gives the border plenty of summer 'body' and tells of much to come in the way of late blooms.

The arrangement looks random at first sight but there is careful discipline here. All the key principles of planting are adhered to, with a strong framework of plants covering the wall and with freestanding buddleja, sorbus and *Rosa chinenesis* 'Mutabilis'. Infill plants, with their varying foliage, create a pleasing understorey and there are such special additions such as the vividly coloured tigridias and shapely

▲ *Tigridia pavonia* is a South African relative of the iris, with brilliantly coloured but somewhat short-lived three-part blooms.

◄ This relaxed, informal border seems to contain plants of almost every size, from alpines to trees. The scarlet bergamot, placed just in front of the pale, variegated foliage of *Phlox paniculata* 'Norah Leigh', makes a dramatic focal point, with a grey-leaved, purple-blue buddleja nearby to soften the effect. The hue of the buddleja flowers recurs, darker in the tall lobelias to its left and then paler to the right, where violet-blue penstemons create an exciting contrast to the fuchsias. Clematis and honeysuckle and an old China rose grace the back wall, creating a harmonious partnership and a fitting backdrop for the rest of the planting.

crinums to act as a focus for the eye. Though colour is abundant, there is also plenty of green to tone down any fussiness and a careful balance of hues at every level.

Other seasons are well catered for, with evergreen box to support the low plants in the foreground and, close to the wall, a rowan tree which will produce spring blossom, autumn berries and a stately outline. Gentle gradations of height make this border easy on the eye, but the colours give plenty of summer excitement.

Planting Plan   5m x 2.5m (16ft x 8ft)

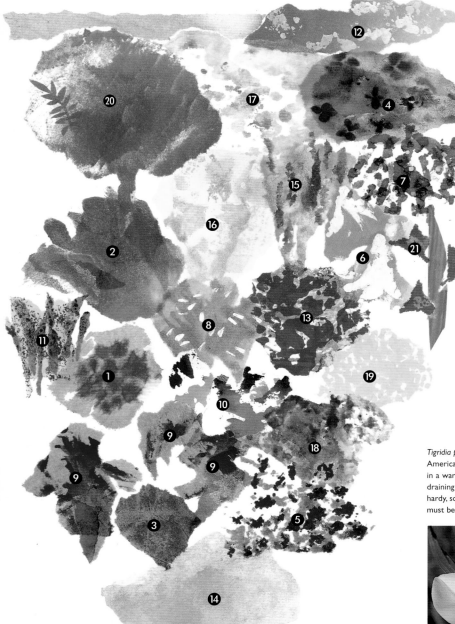

Key	Plant	Qty/Space (cm)	Substitute
①	Aster novae-angliae	3 /60	A. frikartii 'Mönch'
②	Buddleja davidii 'Nanho Blue'	1 /250	B. fallowiana
③	Buxus balearica	1 /45	B. sempervirens
④	Clematis viticella 'Rubra'	1 /120	C. 'Royal Velours'
⑤	Campanula carpatica	3 /30	Viola cornuta
⑥	Crinum powellii	3 /90	Amaryllis belladonna
⑦	Fuchsia 'Lady Betty Spens'	3 /75	F. 'Mrs Popple'
⑧	Galtonia candicans	10 /45	G. princeps
⑨	Iris germanica	5 /45	Sisyrinchium striatum
⑩	Iris sibirica	3 /90	I. spuria
⑪	Lobelia x gerardii 'Vedrariensis'	3 /45	L. 'Russian Princess'
⑫	Lonicera japonica 'Halliana'	1 /120	L. 'Graham Thomas'
⑬	Monarda 'Cambridge Scarlet'	1 /75	Salvia microphylla
⑭	Origanum vulgare 'Aureum'	5 /30	Mentha x gracilis 'Aurea'
⑮	Penstemon 'Sour Grapes'	3 /45	P. 'Stapleford Gem'
⑯	Phlox paniculata 'Norah Leigh'	3 /60	P. 'Harlequin'
⑰	Rosa chinensis var. mutabilis	1 /150	R. 'Hermosa'
⑱	Rosmarinus 'Severn Sea'	1 /90	Salix subopposita
⑲	Santolina rosmarinifolia 'Primrose Gem'	1 /60	S. pinnata 'Edward Bowles'
⑳	Sorbus aucuparia	1 /600	S. hupehensis
㉑	Tigridia pavonia	5 /20	

Qty: *the number of specimens used in this recipe; numbers can be adjusted to suit a different site.*
Space: *recommended spacings for optimum growth (in centimetres).*

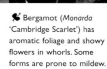

Tigridia pavonia, a South American species, is happiest in a warm, sunny spot in free-draining soil. It is not frost-hardy, so in cold areas bulbs must be replanted in spring.

Tall-growing *Lobelia x gerardii* 'Vedrariensis' is a perennial which prefers moist, rich soil. Though short-lived, it is easy to reproduce from seed.

🍃 Bergamot (*Monarda* 'Cambridge Scarlet') has aromatic foliage and showy flowers in whorls. Some forms are prone to mildew.

◄ Blue and gold is a classic colour combination, achieved here by planting the deep blue *Campanula carpatica* among the golden leaves of *Origanum vulgare* 'Aureum'. Both can be clipped back in midsummer, to foster new growth.

Groundwork: Dense planting aids in preserving soil structure and in conserving moisture, but for such lush growth, in so well-lit a spot, it will be necessary to feed the soil and to mulch it each year with rotted compost. The foreground plants, particularly the golden marjoram and cotton lavender, are happy in very dry conditions, but the taller perennials, particularly the bergamot, phlox and lobelia, prefer rich, moist soil.

Planting procedure: The permanent plants will take a few seasons to fill out and create such a lush planting. For speedy results, begin by planting the marjoram, campanula and penstemons up to 20cm (8in) apart. After their first season, you may be able to do a little thinning – perhaps saving the plants you remove for elsewhere. An interesting alternative would be to introduce such temporary plants as clarkias, stocks or nigella for the first summer, to fill gaps while the larger subjects establish themselves. You could add gladiolus, lilies or alliums to the galtonias for bursts of first-season colour.

Maintenance: Buddlejas, vigorous shrubs, need an annual prune practically to ground level. Tender plants, such as the fuchsias and, in cold locations, the penstemons, must be replaced each spring. The gaps they leave could be filled with spring bulbs like tulips or fritillaries or such early-flowering biennials as wallflowers or drumstick primulas.

Future: The dividing line between a well-stocked and an overcrowded border is a fine one. Some of the perennials will need thinning down within a couple of seasons and, as the rowan tree increases in size and spread, there will be an opportunity to widen the selection with plants that are happy in dappled shade.

❧ *Buddleja davidii*
Butterfly bush. Vigorous and sometimes coarse-growing shrubs with silvery-grey leaves whose undersides are downy. Large panicles of fragrant flowers in the violet to blue range come into bloom after the longest day. Cultivars include 'Black Knight' (deep purple), 'Royal Red', 'Empire Blue' and the intensely floriferous 'Dartmoor'. Adored by butterflies. Cut plants back very hard at winter's end.

❧ *Campanula carpatica*
A low-growing species of bellflower forming compact mounds of foliage up to 20cm (8in) high, furnished with a long run of large, open, bell-shaped flowers during summer. Best cultivars include 'Blue Clips', 'White Clips' and 'Bressingham White'. Easy to divide, indestructible and long in bloom.

❧ *Galtonia*
Summer-flowering bulbs with large, bell-like flowers arranged on stems in the manner of a hyacinth, but more pendulous. *G. candicans* grows to almost 1m (3ft) with waxy white, nodding blooms which hang like bells around the stem. *G. princeps* grows less tall and has greenish-white flowers.

❧ *Monarda*
Bergamot. North American native perennials with creeping rootstocks and aromatic leaves used to flavour Earl Grey tea. Four-sided, 1m (3ft) high branched stems are topped with whorls of ragged flowers. Fine garden forms include 'Cambridge Scarlet', 'Croftway Pink' and the dark-stemmed, purple-bloomed 'Prairie Night'. Happier in moist, well-fed soil than in dry.

❧ *Origanum vulgare*
Marjoram. Valuable herb, native to Europe, with an aroma similar to that of common thyme, but less rank. A slowly creeping rootstock results in mats of fresh green – or golden-green, in the case of *O. v.* 'Aureum' – rounded and sometimes curled leaves. Stems extend to around 45cm (18in) in summer, producing clusters of pale lilac to purple flowers. Cut back stems frequently to ensure plenty of fresh, bright foliage. The flowers are loved by bees.

❧ *Penstemon*
North American members of the foxglove family with tubular flowers in clean, bright colours, sometimes with white or contrasting colours in their throats. Of the hundreds of excellent garden forms, varieties with the narrowest leaves and flowers, such as the pale pink 'Evelyn', are hardiest. In the larger-flowered range are 'Alice Hindley' (lilac-mauve) and 'Sour Grapes' (greenish-blue and purple).

❧ *Santolina rosmarinifolia*
Green cotton lavender. A compact shrub, growing about 45cm (18in) high with a 60cm (2ft) spread, fine but somewhat leathery, emerald-green foliage and primrose-yellow button-shaped flowers. Needs cutting back into the green basal foliage as the flowers fade. Where old plants have become splayed with age, cut back even harder but take cuttings first.

❧ *Penstemon hartwegii*, one of the reddest species of penstemon, is probably the source of colour in such varieties as 'Firebird,' 'Garnet' and 'King George'. Propagate from cuttings, taken in summer.

❧ The pale yellow, button flowers of *Santolina rosmarinifolia* 'Primrose Gem' make a strong contrast with purple violas, which are long in bloom.

AN ALPINE GARDEN

▶ Mediterranean wildflowers, in either their pure wild state or as selected garden forms, have been popular among alpine gardeners for centuries. The wild Greek iris (*Iris pumila*) has been used to develop a huge range of dwarf bearded irises like these.

Raised beds, gravel, old stone troughs furnished with mature lichens and an intriguing collection of plants help compose a classic alpine garden. Such important practical considerations as sharp drainage and full light are taken care of in this design. Retained beds and containers, as well as making it easier for the water to run away, enable even the smallest of plants to be enjoyed at close quarters.

▶ It is late spring in the alpine garden, with rock roses in full bloom, soon to be followed by a steady succession of small but intense bursts of colour. In the foreground gravel, a poppy is about to unfurl; there are cranesbills and irises both flowering and in bud; an evergreen hellebore promises off-season flowers for next winter and tiny hardy cyclamen will pop up in the autumn.

Mountain plants may be small – it is often windy high up and they have to keep their heads down! – but what they lack in stature, they make up for in beauty. Some of the most intense colours are to be found among alpines – the penetrating blue of gentians or the startling cerise of *Geranium cinereum* – and, in a garden, such plants make a sparkling contribution. Beautiful in habit as well as in flower, many alpine plants form small mounds, whereas others will develop ground-hugging mats of foliage and flower.

In this low-profile garden, stone creates the hard structure, backed by high boundary walls and by the taller herbaceous plants – dark tulips and similarly hued bearded irises, with bright yellow asphodeline as a backdrop. The understorey consists of a rich miscellany of alpine plants whose role is to soften the hard surfaces and to 'naturalize' the scene. In a natural mountain landscape, exposed rocks and stony screes occur among the plants and an alpine garden looks more attractive and authentic if a similar effect is achieved.

Ingredients

Key	Plant	Qty / Space (cm)	Substitute
①	Armeria maritima	1 /20	Saponaria ocymoides
②	Asphodeline lutea	3 /45	A. liburnica
③	Dianthus deltoides	1 /30	Gypsophila repens
④	Geranium cinereum var. subcaulescens	1 /20	G. c. 'Ballerina'
⑤	Helleborus argutifolius	1 /75	H. foetidus Wester Flisk Group
⑥	Helianthemum cv	1 /30	Any red helianthemum
⑦	Helianthemum 'Fire Dragon'	1 /30	H. 'Mrs C.W. Earle'
⑧	Iris 'Wren'	5 /30	I. 'Curlew'
⑨	Papaver lateritium	1 /30	P. atlanticum
⑩	Picea mariana 'Nana'	1 /60	Juniperus communis 'Compressa'
⑪	Saxifraga 'Kathleen Pinsent'	1 /20	S. 'Southside Seedling'
⑫	Sempervivum arachnoideum	1 container /10	S. tectorum
⑬	Sempervivum tectorum	1 container /10	Sedum spathulifolium
⑭	Thymus serpyllum	1 /30	T. 'Doone Valley'
⑮	Tulipa 'Queen of Night'	20 /10	T. 'Black Parrot'
⑯	Tulipa tarda	10 /10	T. orphanidea 'Whitallii Group'
⑰	Viola sororia	>3 /20	V. 'Freckles'

Qty: the number of specimens used in this recipe; numbers can be adjusted to suit a different site.
Space: recommended spacings for optimum growth (in centimetres).

✂ A prostrate habit with evergreen, often silvery foliage and a long period of highly coloured blooms make helianthemums one of the alpinist's staple shrubs. Cut back after flowering to promote bushy young growth.

✂ Wild thyme, both aromatic and colourful, is not only a favourite with gardeners: the flowers are ialso irresistible to bees and give their honey a distinctive flavour.

✂ Cranesbills, valuable as larger perennials, also have beautiful alpine relatives. G. cinereum, with its lovely blooms, is one of the easiest species to grow.

Groundwork: Raised beds and containers for alpines need to be free-draining. A layer of broken crocks beneath the compost will assist drainage in containers; a layer of hardcore and the provision of seepage holes are essential at the base of raised beds. The soil must be porous but should have body and enough nourishment to keep plants healthy.

Planting procedure: The tall plants, more suited to lowland conditions, create a lush background which makes a pleasing contrast to the true alpines. Plant tulips at least 10cm (4in) deep in autumn, arranging them in tight groups, with no more than about 10cm (4in) between bulbs. The bearded irises and other perennials should also be planted densely, with spacings of up to 30cm (12in).

Plant the saxifrage, *Geranium cinereum*, thrift and helianthemums close, but not hard up against one another, to show each plant's individual outline. Add at least one winter evergreen per container – here, a dwarf conifer. A dressing of coarse grit reduces the risk of excessive water around plant necks and improves the appearance of an alpine bed.

Maintenance: Control weeds by hand rather than by hoeing or digging.

Planting Plan 2.5m x 8m (8ft x 26ft)

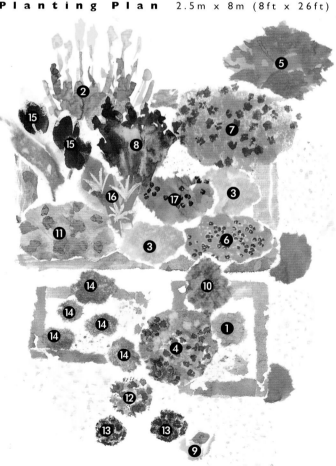

PLANT DIRECTORY

✂ *Geranium cinereum*
A beautiful cranesbill from the Pyrenees, which forms neat rosettes of rounded, deeply lobed foliage, about 20cm by 20cm (8in by 8in). In spring and summer, pale pink flowers with darker veining open cup-shaped, but flatten as they mature. Even more spectacular and more vigorous is the Turkish subspecies, *G. c.* var. *subcaulescens*, whose flowers are a vivid rosy-magenta.

✂ *Helianthemum*
Sun rose, Rock rose. Low-growing, evergreen shrubs with narrow, simple leaves and terminal sprays of short-lived blooms. Colours range from deep red, through pink and yellow to white. Three species, *H. nummularium*, *H. appeninum* and *H. croceum*, have given rise to such hybrids as 'Raspberry Ripple', which is pink and white, 'Mrs C.W. Earle', a double red, and 'Ben Heckla', which is startling orange.

✂ *Saxifraga* (Ligulatae group)
The silver saxifrages have matted rosettes of foliage encrusted with a silvery or limy deposit; in spring and early summer their flowers are carried on showy panicles. Beautiful examples are 'Kathleen Pinsent', whose sprays of starry flowers are rose-pink, 'Tumbling Waters', which produces huge, arching panicles of pure white, foamy blossom and 'Southside Seedling', which bears bicoloured pink and white blooms on generous sprays.

✂ *Thymus serpyllum*
Wild thyme. A mat-forming plant with wiry stems, tiny dark green leaves and, in early summer, a thick covering of small, fragrant, mauve to pink blooms. Evergreen, its foliage may burnish in autumn frosts. Garden forms include 'Pink Chintz' and 'Snowdrift'.

A BOWER GARDEN

► *Phlox paniculata* is one of the most colourful of the taller summer perennials, making a bold display from a distance but adding further delight close-to, not only because of the individual beauty of the flowers but also for its sweet, honey-like fragrance. This variety is 'Cool of the Evening'.

A strong emphasis on vertical planting creates a lofty display in this relatively small area, with a welter of lush greenery and gorgeous flower colours. Archways provide the structural framework, furnished with several varieties of clematis which soften the effect with their foliage and add to the richness of the planting with their flowers. Purples, maroons and wine-pinks make up the principal colours, but these are contrasted with pale yellow flowers and harmonized with silvery foliage.

► Clematis, like honeysuckle, is the perfect bower plant – hence its colloquial name, virgin's bower – and varieties here have been chosen to harmonize colours. On the right, the bold maroon flowers of the viticella clematis 'Polish Spirit' reach across to mingle with *C. x triternata*, whose spindly sepals turn pale at their centres. Behind, one of the *C. texensis* varieties, 'Etoile Rose', produces deep rose-pink, tulip-shaped blossoms. In a startling textural contrast to all the lushness, the pot-grown cordyline gives substance to the soft design. Its spiky foliage is evergreen, making it a central anchoring plant, very valuable in winter when the climbers are in eclipse.

▲ Few other perennials
are so tall, or have such
a lengthy flowering
period as hollyhocks.
Used as foreground
plants here, they help to
reinforce the sense of
height. Hollyhocks are
prone to rust disease: if
this becomes a problem,
you could substitute
mulleins (*Verbascum*).

Summer produces such a mass of exuberant growth that the bower's metal arches all but disappear beneath the greenery. But the framework still works to hold the planting together. The bower plants soften, but do not dilute, its structural value.

Hard paving and cobbles, besides giving an easy footway, make a firm base from which the greenery can spring, but everywhere the edges are blurred and softened with ground-level plants that crowd in on each other and spill on to the paths, their softness making a contrast with the hard stone. And even among these more lowly plants, cameo dramas are acting themselves out: spiky iris leaves contrast with the soft, felty foliage of *Stachys byzantina*; there are pinks about to flower at the feet of the mighty hollyhock and, right at the back, the view to the house is softened by sprays of *Crambe cordifolia* going to seed.

This is very much a 'planting for the season', but one that will last for the entire second half of summer. The season could be extended by introducing early- and late-flowering climbers – more clematis, perhaps, including *C. alpina* for spring, and even the winter-flowering *C. cirrhosa* var. *balearica* – as well as spring and autumn perennials. But the real success of this planting lies in the intensity of its late-summer climax and nothing should be done to dilute that moment of glory.

Groundwork: To achieve this height and spread in a season, enrich the soil with rotted manure or compost before planting. Mulches help to reduce evaporation from bare soil while the ground cover gets established.

Planting procedure: Once the framework is erected, begin by planting the shrubs and climbers. Clematis need deep, fertile soil and cool roots and will therefore benefit from a dressing of bonemeal at the planting hole and a thick mulch to retain moisture.

Group the low plants right at the feet of the tall hollyhocks to effect a sudden change in plant height. There is no gentle grading of size here: the aim is for maximum drama.

Maintenance: In this confined space, be ready to restrict the size of some perennials by lifting, dividing and replanting a portion of the original plant every few years. Do not worry if some of the plants knit together to make a complete ground cover, provided weaker ones do not get smothered; the planting will look more natural too.

Hollyhocks are short-lived perennials and will need replacing every few years: collect seed to grow into replacement plants. Feed plants once annually, but keep topping up the organic content of the soil by returning compost to it. Keep the planting fresh during summer by pulling away dead and dying flowers; if cut hard back, hollyhocks sometimes produce secondary stems later. The cordyline will not tolerate severe frost and neither will its container. Give both winter protection if your climate is harsh.

Strict discipline is essential in so small an area, particularly with the more rumbustious climbers, to regulate their size and habit so that neighbours are not squashed and the form and structure are retained. Tie in all young shoots as they develop, particularly in spring and early summer. Prune all viticella clematis very hard back in late winter.

Future: Consider broadening the season a little by introducing later-flowering climbers.

Planting Plan   Arch 2.5m x 2.5m (8ft x 8ft); total area 4m x 4m (13ft x 13ft)

❧ Hybrids of *Clematis viticella* begin blooming soon after the longest day and should stay in flower until the end of the growing season. This variety is 'Royal Velours'.

Sea holly – this one is a fine form of *Eryngium alpinum* – is blessed with many important attributes: distinctive outline, rich blue-grey foliage and an eye-catching, spiky flower shape.

❧ 'Etoile Rose' is one of the finest varieties bred from the herbaceous species *Clematis texensis*. The pale-edged carmine sepals turn outwards at their tips, creating a tulip-like elegance

Ingredients

Key	Plant	Qty/Space (cm)	Substitute
①	Alcea rosea 'Lemon Light'	3 /90	A. rugosa
②	Artemisia 'Powis Castle'	3 /45	A. absinthium 'Lambrook Silver'
③	Buxus sempervirens 'Suffruticosa'	7 /45	Sarcococca humilis
④	Crambe cordifolia	I	Thalictrum flavum
⑤	Clematis × triternata 'Rubromarginata'	I /150	C. 'Minuet'
⑥	Clematis 'Etoile Rose'	I /150	C. 'Gravetye Beauty'
⑦	Clematis 'Perle d'Azur'	I /150	C 'Hagley Hybrid'
⑧	Clematis 'Polish Spirit'	I /150	C. 'Etoile Violette'
⑨	Cordyline australis 'Torbay Dazzler'	I /150	C. a. 'Torbay Red'
⑩	Diascia rigescens	>I /30	Nemesia caerulea
⑪	Dianthus 'Laced Monarch'	3 /45	D. 'Camilla', D. 'Dad's Favourite'
⑫	Iris germanica	6 /60	Any iris (yellow, blue or purple)
⑬	Leymus arenarius	3 /30	Helichtrotrichon sempervirens
⑭	Linum narbonense	6 /30	L. perenne
⑮	Phlox paniculata 'Cool of the Evening'	I /75	P. p. 'Windsor', P. p. 'Eve Cullum'
⑯	Phlox 'White Admiral'	I /75	P. 'Fujiyama'
⑰	Stachys byzantina	3 /45	S. b. 'Primrose Heron'

Qty: the number of specimens used in this recipe; numbers can be adjusted to suit a different site.
Space: recommended spacings for optimum growth (in centimetres).

Notes: There are more than 400 different kinds of clematis to choose from for this kind of display, but to keep the mood and style similar, go for smaller-flowered viticella and texensis hybrids, rather than too many with large blooms.

Almost any variety of honeysuckle could be made to blend with the clematis.

The addition of bulbs for spring and winter will extend the season.

▲ Invaluable as an architectural plant, the New Zealand cabbage palm (*Cordyline australis*) grows for many years with all its spiky foliage radiating from the top of a single stem. Slow-growing, it adapts perfectly to life in a container.

❧ Like the mallows to which they are related, hollyhocks have stamens fused to form a central spike. The yellow colouring in garden hybrids comes from *Alcea rugosa*, itself an excellent garden plant.

A light, airy combination in soft, pastel shades is provided here by blending lavender-pink South African diascias with the soft azure of the flax (*Linum narbonense*).

❧ The leaves of lamb's ears (*Stachys byzantina*) are clothed with thick, white, felty hairs, making this a valuable ground-cover plant for enriching the texture of a planting scheme.

PLANT DIRECTORY

❧ Alcea
Hollyhock. Rugged perennials from Europe and the Middle East. *Alcea rugosa* has primrose-yellow flowers on more slender stems than the better-known *A. rosea* which is pink in the wild, but cultivars have been bred to produce blooms in yellow, apricot, white, pink, red and aubergine. Double-flowered varieties include Chater's Double Group and 'Peaches and Dreams'.

❧ Clematis viticella hybrids
One of three most valuable clematis groups. The species, a European native, has small blue flowers from the second half of summer onwards. Hybridization has resulted in a full range of hues from deep red through blues and purples to paler pinks and pure white; all varieties are highly floriferous. Prune hard back each winter.

❧ Cordyline australis
Leathery, strap-like leaves emerge from a woody central stem which slowly extends with age until a small tree is formed. In mild areas, where plants reach maturity, large sprays of very small, sweetly fragrant flowers appear in spring, followed by small fruits in summer. Varieties with coloured foliage include the dark purple 'Atropurpurea', bronzy-red 'Torbay Red' and variegated 'Torbay Dazzler'.

❧ Dianthus
Pink. A valuable genus with blue-grey, spiky foliage and fragrant flowers, with antique varieties as well as modern hybrids. For border use, modern hybrids such as 'Doris', pink and carmine, and 'Diane', salmon-orange, tend to repeat flower. Old varieties like 'London Brocade' and 'Sops in Wine' do not repeat but come in beautiful combinations of maroon or purple laced with white or pale mauve.

❧ Iris germanica
Bearded iris. Rhizome-forming perennials valuable for their strap-like foliage as well as the early summer display of large, colourful, often fragrant flowers. Parts of the flowers are arranged in threes, giving the classic iris or 'fleur de lys' shape. Almost every colour is represented, apart from red, often in pleasing two-tone combinations. To flower well, irises need full sun and free-draining soil which allows the rhizomes to bake in summer.

❧ Phlox paniculata
Flowers of the traditional herbaceous border. Bold panicles of honey-scented flowers are produced in mid- to late summer, in some startling colour ranges that include vivid orange-red, as in 'Firefly', soft shades of lilac-mauve, 'Amethyst', pink and white bicolor, and the handsome pure white 'Fujiyama'. Divide regularly.

❧ Stachys byzantina
Lamb's ears. Ground-cover perennial with creeping rhizomes and basal leaves thickly clothed in felty, silver-grey hairs. The flower spikes are as downy as the leaves, and carry small, dark red lipped flowers. Happiest on free-draining soil in full sun.

A TASTE OF THE TROPICS

▶ A happy combination of exotic species from opposite sides of the world. New Zealand flax (*Phormium tenax*) associates here with *Malvastrum lateritium*, a ground-trailing native from South America.

It can be fun to bring a sense of the exotic into a garden – especially a temperate one – by developing a tropical summer planting. In this short-term border, bananas, New Zealand flax and heat-loving species from Central America form the basis of the planting. Hot, strong colours enhance the fiesta atmosphere and there is plenty of bold, giant foliage to build up the jungle effect. Though destined to last but a single summer, every plant here will flower non-stop from late spring until the first of the frosts or, with its foliage, will look decorative for even longer.

Although there is a permanent framework to this border, consisting of clipped trees and a backdrop hedge, in a temperate climate the bulk of the planting must be renewed each season. None of the tender plants will survive unless lifted and overwintered in a greenhouse, or unless cuttings are taken to develop new plants for the next year. Though this creates work, it is a great way to widen the planting opportunities.

◄ Hot tropics! This border is in a garden where frosts can be sharp and where cold, penetrating winds are considered normal in winter. And yet, a lush tropical feel has been conjured up simply by arranging tender plants for a bright and cheerful summer display. Few of the plants here are frost-hardy, but since they grow so rapidly, and because their flowering period is long, they give an impression of maturity just a few weeks after planting.

▲ The blue-flowered *Solanum rantonnetii* and *Abutilon* 'Souvenir de Bonn' grow rapidly, flower very young and go on flowering. All these are important qualities in cold climates, where tropical subjects must be planted each spring.

Tropical plants tend to have dramatic, oversized foliage, so using such species as banana, canna or big grasses helps to create the sense of lushness. In cold gardens, you can cheat by using tropical-looking plants that are more hardy than they appear. *Rheum palmatum*, for example, has shapely architectural foliage and for a more spiky, desert look you could select yuccas or cordylines.

Deciding what to do with such a border in winter and spring can pose problems, unless you are a devotee of spring bedding: plants such as primroses, pansies or spring bulbs may be planted in autumn to perform during these leaner seasons then be banished, after flowering, to make room for the return of the tropicals in early summer the following year.

Planting Plan   3.5m x 10m (12ft x 33ft)

Ingredients

Key	Plant	Qty/Space (cm)	Substitute
①	Abutilon 'Souvenir de Bonn'	1 /150	A. 'Ashford Red'
②	Argyranthemum 'Jamaica Primrose'	3 /60	A. 'Cornish Gold'
③	Canna 'Striata'	1 /90	C. 'Rosemond Coles'
④	Cordyline australis 'Purpurea'	<5 /100	C. 'Torbay Dazzler'
⑤	Dahlia 'Glorie van Heemstede'	5 /90	D. 'Davenport Delight'
⑥	Dahlia 'Preston Park'	5 /90	D. 'Bishop of Llandaff'
⑦	Diascia barbarae 'Ruby Field'	>3 /45	D. rigescens
⑧	Eccremocarpus scaber	1 /120	Mina lobata
⑨	Eucalyptus gunnii	1 /900	E. niphophila
⑩	Lathyrus odoratus	>3 /60	L. tingitanus
⑪	Lobelia cardinalis	5 /45	L. x vedrariensis
⑫	Lobelia tupa	3 /100	Salvia involucrata
⑬	Ligustrum lucidum 'Excelsum Superbum'	3 /200	Prunus lusitanica
⑭	Musa acuminata	1 /150	Ensete ventricosum
⑮	Pericallis lanata	1 /45	Senecio pulcher
⑯	Phormium cookianum	1 /120	Yucca gloriosa
⑰	Salvia confertiflora	3 /120	S. microphylla
⑱	Solanum rantonnetii	1 /140	S. crispum
⑲	Verbena bonariensis	3 /90	Gaura lindheimeri

Qty: the number of specimens used in this recipe; numbers can be adjusted to suit a different site.
Space: recommended spacings for optimum growth (in centimetres).

An exciting combination of brilliant foliage from *Canna* 'Striata' contrasting with the dark leaves and scarlet flowers of *Lobelia cardinalis*.

Groundwork: To sustain the rapid summer growth of these plants the soil must be enriched at planting time with manure or a generous dressing of artificial fertilizer or one composed of blood, fish and bonemeal. Moisture is important too, particularly while the plants are establishing: a thick mulch will help to seal in the moisture. Be prepared to irrigate, especially during the initial stages, if drought is forecast.

Planting procedure: This is as close as gardening gets to an instant border. Many of the plants will already be flowering when they are planted; others will develop with surprising speed. It is important, therefore, to have a carefully devised planting plan and to stick as closely as possible to the planned spacings. Permanent outline plants – the hedge at the back, the standard ligustrum trees and the phormium – cannot be moved and will dictate the position of everything else. Make sure that such key specimens as the banana, abutilons, cannas and sweet-pea tower are placed well and that all the lesser plants are in a good position in relation to the outline. Be ready to thin out one or two plants if their growth is too vigorous.

◄ Bronze, sword-like foliage and a distinctly upright habit make this cordyline contrast strongly with the soft green-and-cream palmate leaves of *Abutilon* 'Souvenir de Bonn.'

Maintenance: Pick over the planting regularly, removing dead and dying blooms. This is important after wet spells, not only to prevent unsightliness and promote more flowering but to remove sources of possible disease. Make feeding a regular routine: use a high-potassium liquid feed at least once every two weeks or apply slow-release granules according to the manufacturer's instructions.

Future: Purchasing new plants each season would be costly, but propagating new young specimens and overwintering them is an economical way of ensuring continuity. Marginally hardy plants can be left in the ground and protected with bulky mulches where frosts are light to moderate.

PLANT DIRECTORY

❧ *Argyranthemum*
Marguerite. Shrubby plants from the daisy family, native in Madeira and the Canary Islands, and seldom without blooms, even in winter. To keep them fresh, cut back at regular intervals during the growing season. They can be grown into hedges, trained as standards or simply cut back repeatedly and treated like perennials. Best varieties include 'Jamaica Primrose' (yellow) 'Vancouver' (pink) and the species *A. foeniculaceum* whose white flowers have gold centres. All are frost-tender but will root from cuttings.

❧ *Eccremocarpus scaber*
Chilean glory flower. Vigorous herbaceous climber, to 3m (10ft) or more, with generous clusters of long, tubular flowers in orange, red, yellow or pink. Barely frost-hardy, but quick to multiply from self-sown seedlings. The rootstock is perennial.

❧ *Eucalyptus*
Gum tree. This huge Australasian genus provides valuable trees that are also useful, when immature, as foliage plants. *E. gunnii* is one of the toughest and, if pruned hard, will produce juvenile foliage which is rounded and covered in a mealy bloom that makes it appear silver-white. When grown to maturity, the adult leaves are barely less handsome, being up to 15cm (6in) long and richly aromatic.

❧ *Lobelia tupa*
From Chile, a huge relative of the humble bedding lobelia, with bold, lance-shaped leaves and robust, reddish flower stems, furnished along their length with curious parrot-bill blooms midway between orange and brick red. Not totally frost-hardy, but in a mild garden it will survive if protected with a bulky winter mulch over the crowns.

❧ *Salvia confertiflora*
An architectural perennial, excellent for outline but with flowers that are somewhat understated. Stems grow to 1m (3ft) or more, with big, nettle-like leaves and, in the second half of summer, rat-tail flowers in rusty-red. This Brazilian native dislikes it too dry but needs sunshine to coax it into bloom.

❧ *Solanum rantonnetii*
A potato bush from South America, growing to around 2m (6ft) high with dark stems and bottle-green, simple leaves. The flowers, produced all through summer, are disc-like, with star-shaped seams in the petals which vary in colour from deep mauve to pale blue. The variety 'Royal Robe' has rich purple flowers with a bright yellow eye.

❧ *Verbena bonariensis*
A favourite with butterflies and suitable for the border front despite its height, because the stems are so thin they will not mask shorter plants behind. The tall, four-sided and much branched stems grow to 2m (6ft) or more, with narrow leaves rough to the touch, and clusters of flowers in bright purple-mauve. Barely frost-hardy but a prolific seeder, so spring-germinated plants should survive.

❧ The extraordinary parrot-bill flowers of *Lobelia tupa* appear in mid- to late summer on spikes that reach 120cm (4ft). In cold areas, this plant needs winter protection.

Though hardly a tropical plant, the strong – almost violent – purple and the rich fragrance of the pea-flower (*Lathyrus odoratus*), make it a worthy occupant of this border for exotics.

ROMANTIC COUNTRY RETREAT

A dreamy country garden, seen here in late summer, is full of colour and rich with different plant species, yet it makes a quiet statement. The choice of plants ensures not only a soft but striking outline but also a long run of colour, sustained from spring, when alliums and other bulbs are in flower, all through summer and deep into autumn. The plants work hard in this composition, providing interesting seedheads as well as fresh bloom: they are seen now, gently bringing the colours down to autumn russet and dun as the days get shorter.

▲ The seedheads of *Allium cristophii* look like exploding fireworks among the greenish-white blooms of *Astrantia major*. Behind them, a pink poppy and double-flowered meadow cranesbills provide late-summer colour.

► Shimmering and waving in the breeze, the giant oat plant makes an eye-catching summer display, especially when its parchment-coloured blooms are contrasted with the reddish foliage of the cotinus behind. Distinctive, almost translucent thorns on the *Rosa sericea* add further interest and will be important later in the year, when it forms a handsome silhouette. With the clipped holly as a formal centrepiece and the high, sheltering backdrop planting, outline and framework plants both decorate and protect, making a perfect setting for the perennials and annuals.

Two distinctly architectural plants create the framework for this planting, both serving a very different purpose but working together in harmony. The holly (*Ilex aquifolium* 'Madame Briot'), clipped formally into a whorled shape, creates a distinctive structure which offsets the natural effect of the rest of the planting. In winter, the holly will become the main feature, standing out among the declining perennials and ready to make a sparkling centrepiece for the first of the spring bulbs. In the foreground, a giant oat

creates a summer focal point, making sharp angles with its flower stems and filling the space with a shimmering, misty shower of papery inflorescences. They move to and fro in the breeze, adding an extra dimension to an already fascinating border.

The herbaceous plants selected for the richly varied understorey in this planting are either wild species, or similar to them in appearance, including cranesbills, wild poppies, decorative garlics and other wayside plants. Large-flowered hybrid plants would

be out of place in so naturalistic a planting. But because such perennials as cranesbills and astrantia tend to lack a firm outline, it has been necessary to provide a strong background of trees and shrubs with distinctive foliage.

Planting Plan   7m x 4m (23ft x 13ft)

▲ It is possible to purchase hollies ready clipped and trained like this, but they can be expensive. It is more fun to train your own, though it will take time. You will need to get the plants to the desired height first, before you begin your sculpting. Clip once a year, in early spring, just before the new growth begins.

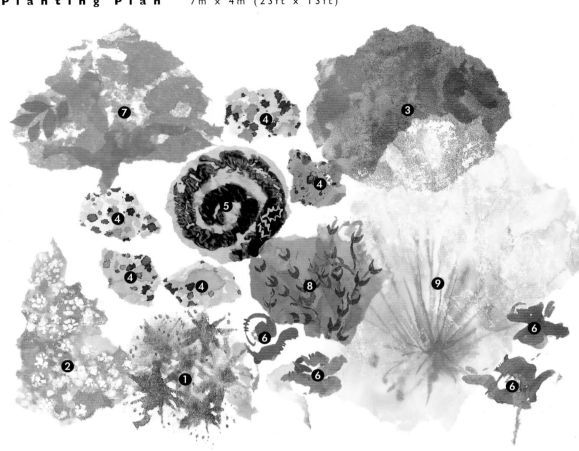

❧ Purple-leaved smoke bush (*Cotinus coggygria* 'Royal Purple') grows larger leaves with stronger colours if pruned hard back every second year.

Selected forms of wild European meadow cranesbill include this handsome double-flowered variety, *Geranium pratense* 'Plenum Violaceum'.

❧ This lovely winter-flowering cherry (*Prunus x subhirtella* 'Autumnalis') blooms from leaf fall, seen here, until the new leaves open in spring.

❧ Melancholy gentleman (*Astrantia major*) is a relative of the carrot. It flowers here among the leaves of the striped grass, *Miscanthus sinensis* 'Zebrinus'.

❧ Hollies are the most valuable of evergreens for structural planting. Variegated forms like *Ilex aquifolium* 'Madame Briot' are as handsome in leaf as in berry and make a year-round display.

Ingredients

Key	Plant	Qty / Space (cm)	Substitute
①	Allium cristophii (in seed)	>3 /20	A. aflatunense
②	Astrantia major	5 /45	A. maxima
③	Cotinus coggygria 'Royal Purple'	1 /150	C. 'Grace'
④	Geranium pratense 'Plenum Violaceum'	3 /60	G. psilostemon
⑤	Ilex aquifolium 'Madame Briot'	1 /150	Any holly
⑥	Papaver rhoeas	1 pkt seed /20	Shirley poppies; P. r. 'Mother of Pearl'
⑦	Prunus x subhirtella 'Autumnalis'	1 /300	P. 'Kursar'
⑧	Rosa sericea omeiensis f. pteracantha	1 /150	R. 'Highdownensis'
⑨	Stipa gigantea	1 /90	Helictotrichon sempervirens

Here are some alternative or extra plants, all of which would blend comfortably into this relaxed planting but would also flower at different seasons.

Leucojum aestivum	3 /20	Camassia
Allium moly	5 /20	Fritillaria pallida
Lilium martagon 'Album'	3 /45	L. chalcedonicum
Campanula takesimana	1 /45	C. punctata
Achillea 'Lachsschönheit'	1 /60	A. 'Cerise Queen'
Eupatorium rugosum	1 /60	Aruncus dioicus
Aster lateriflorus	1 /60	A. ericoides

Qty: the number of specimens used in this recipe; numbers can be adjusted to suit a different site.
Space: recommended spacings for optimum growth (in centimetres).

Groundwork: Even in a naturalistic design, care is needed to ensure a good balance. Not only should plants look well together when they bloom but there should also be a comfortable proportion of herbaceous plants to outline shrubs and trees. In their early stages, the young shrubs need protecting from strong competition from the perennials, particularly some of the vigorous cranesbills.
Planting procedure: Take great care in positioning the key outline plants. Avoid an awkward line-up – with another tree, perhaps, or a building – when placing the holly and be sure to give a prominent position to the oat and the remaining shrubs. Planting of the herbaceous species, on the other hand, can be as random as you like, matching up their colours in whatever combination pleases you best.

Maintenance: Make sure the soil is weed-free before you begin! Thereafter, allow the plants to seed themselves but pull out unwanted seedlings or invasive varieties.

While fertile soil is essential, you must be careful never to overdo the feeding or to use too thick a mulch. The aim is for most of these plants to reproduce naturally and to resemble their wild counterparts as closely as possible. A single annual feed or light dressing with well-rotted manure will be more than enough.
Future: Inevitably, as the shrubs grow, ground space for the herbaceous plants will diminish. If you wish to keep the shrubs small, or to eliminate one or more of them, this will give more space, but always remember the importance of outline plants in a seemingly random design.

◀ *Stipa gigantea* is an elegant member of the oat tribe whose huge, papery panicles are borne on 2m (6ft) wand-like stems. Their leaf tussocks are evergreen.

PLANT DIRECTORY

❧ *Astrantia major*
Melancholy gentleman. Members of the carrot family, with bunched umbels of flowers held in green and white calyces shaped rather like crowns. In varieties such as 'Hadspen Blood' the flowers are deep maroon; 'Shaggy' has enlarged, shaggy calyces and 'Sunningdale' has variegated foliage.

❧ *Cotinus*
Smoke bush. Medium to large shrub with rounded, smooth leaves – purple in some varieties – and fluffy seedheads which give the impression of smoke. The autumn foliage is superb, especially if plants are pruned back every second year to ensure lush growth. Susceptible to verticillium wilt.

❧ *Ilex aquifolium*
Common holly. Decorative, not only for leaf and berry but also for their winter outline: prickly evergreen foliage, tiny white flowers in spring and handsome berries in winter. Best variegated kinds are 'Madame Briot', 'Silver Queen' and 'Handsworth New Silver'. Hollies adapt well to pruning, either into formal shapes or to keep to a manageable size.

❧ *Papaver rhoeas* 'Mother of Pearl'
One of the prettiest annual series selected from wild field poppies by the English plantsman Cedric Morris. Flower colours range through pearly pinks and white to silvery-grey and sombre maroon. There are picotees and flowers whose colour comes from dense patterns of veining. Weed out dull reds and other undesirable shades that can crop up. Does better on hungry, dryish land than on rich loam.

❧ *Prunus x subhirtella* 'Autumnalis'
Winter-flowering cherry. One of a huge family of ornamental trees, this seldom exceeds 7m (23ft) in height and has an open but rounded outline. White flowers produced during mild spells throughout winter often persist until just before the new leaves appear. There is a pink form, 'Autumnalis Rosea'.

❧ *Stipa gigantea*
Giant oat. A tussock-forming perennial grass with dark green, narrow foliage which is soft to the touch and with tall, wand-like flowering stems – up to 2m (6ft) in height – topped with panicles of oat flowers. On opening, these turn from pale green to a papery parchment colour, catching the light as they tremble in the breeze. Easy to raise from seed or by division.

VARIATIONS ON A POTAGER

▲ Onions, leeks and garlic can be as attractive when they have gone to seed as can the more ornamental alliums. It is important, however, to stick rigidly to crop rotations, since dying onions can carry white rot and infect subsequent crops.

This traditional French *potager* is as artistic as the most sumptuous of ornamental displays, but as hardworking as a commercial kitchen garden. With the cost of space increasing, and the resulting trend for plots to be smaller, it is wise to use the same space for more than one purpose. There is much pleasure to be had from strolling the ordered paths and lingering by the features, whether or not you have a basket to hand for picking.

With skilful design, a productive area can be as beautiful as any part of the garden, while still yielding an abundance of fresh vegetables and fruit. The design in this garden is strictly formal, with brick-paved pathways, neatly clipped box hedges and other topiary making a tight, geometric framework within which the more temporary planting of vegetables takes place. Handsome though the layout is, every hedge and pathway takes up space; therefore, yields per square metre will be lower than in a more intensively planted kitchen garden. If your space is limited, keep the framework simple – perhaps no more than two or four beds with a cruciform path to divide them.

Vegetables need to be grown in full light and rich soil, to be fed frequently and dressed with organic matter. Their maintenance needs are heavy, with annual clips for hedges, twice-yearly pruning for fruit and roses, and almost daily weeding, thinning, planting and harvesting. But the rewards of growing your own produce are tangible.

Rhubarb chard, whose vivid red stems provide strong colours in the kitchen garden, is closely related to beet spinach.

❧ Sweet peas, traditional in a kitchen garden, are grown here on stick wigwams and make a fragrant alternative to climbing beans.

The Cape gooseberry (*Physalis peruviana*) adds character with its edible lantern fruits.

▲ The blue globe thistle (*Echinops ritro*) is irresistible to bees. As it hails from the Caucasus, it is impervious to hard winters but benefits from being lifted and divided every few years.

◄ Once the structure has been laid out, the choice of plants for individual beds is virtually unlimited. Here, sweetcorn has followed early salad crops and gourds are trained on to stick wigwams for a late harvest. Chives and other herbs, arranged in rows or planted in corners, will provide a constant green display as well as a supply of fresh flavourings for the kitchen. Cordon and step-over fruit – apples trained as horizontal espaliers at ankle height – provide structure as well as food and, for long-lasting decoration, there are standard roses and a white-leaved willow.

Planting Plan   min. 2m x 2m (6ft x 6ft)

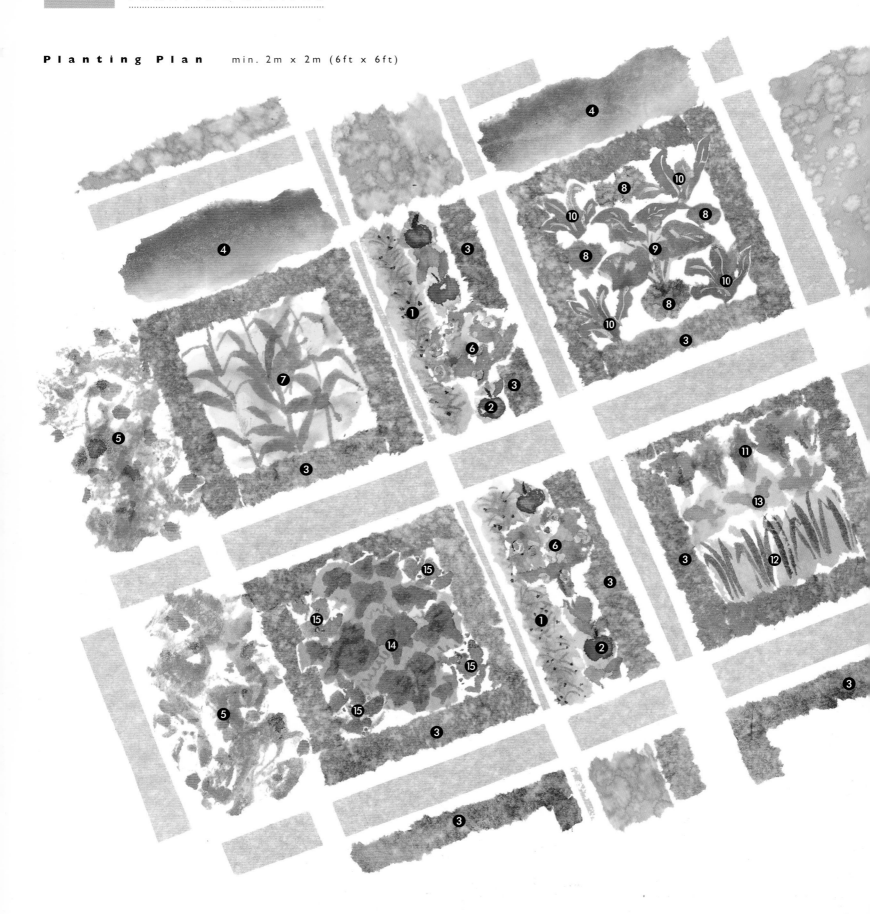

◄ Garlic chives (*Allium nigrum*) is a handsome herbaceous perennial with edible foliage tasting like a mix of garlic and onion. The white flowers look beautiful here, against a background of parsley that has gone to seed. To multiply garlic chives, simply lift and then divide clumps in early spring.

Ingredients

Key Plant	Qty/Space	Substitute
PERMANENT PLANTS to make the framework		
① *Allium schoenoprasum* (chives)	5 per metre	Thyme, sage or violas
② Apples, step-over trained	1 per 2 metres	Cordon soft fruit
③ *Buxus sempervirens* (hedge)	2 per metre	*Rosmarinus officinalis*
④ *Lavandula angustifolia* 'Forescate'	4 per metre	*Teucrium*
⑤ *Lathyrus odoratus* (sweet peas)	as needed	Nasturtiums or runner beans
⑥ standard roses	as required	Standard fuchsias
BED ONE		
⑦ Sweetcorn	5 per metre	
BED TWO		
⑧ Cabbage	2 per metre	
⑨ Kale	2 per metre	
⑩ Calabrese	2 per metre	
BED THREE		
⑪ Garlic	5 per metre	
⑫ Carrots	10 per metre	
⑬ Turnips	10 per metre	
BED FOUR		
⑭ Courgettes/squash	1 per metre	
⑮ French beans	5 per metre	

Qty: *the number of specimens used in this recipe; numbers can be adjusted to suit a different site.*
Space: *recommended spacings for optimum growth.*

▼ A vista down the kitchen garden shows the rustic arch, made from flexed hazel wands. This arch is furnished with sweet peas in flower, but arches could also be used to grow such soft fruits as loganberries and Worcesterberries, or they could have climbing beans trained over them.

CROPPING WITHIN THE BEDS:
A four-year rotation

To discourage disease and achieve maximum yields, crops should be rotated by moving them round clockwise, into the next bed, each year. This leaves an optimum interval of four seasons before the same vegetables are grown on the same land. A simple potager divided into four sections, or beds, thus provides for a perfect cropping plan.
Below are some typical crop rotation ideas.

Bed 1/Year 1
Sweetcorn/maincrop potatoes
OR early salad crops followed by late root crops

Bed 2/Year 2
Legumes (peas and beans), including some autumn-sown broad beans, French beans, dwarf peas and possibly mangetouts or sugar peas

Bed 3/Year 3
Cabbage family, including broccoli or kale for early spring, spring cabbages for early summer, Brussels sprouts and winter cauliflower or Savoy cabbages

Bed 4/Year 4
Root crops: carrots, parsnips, Hamburg parsley, salsify, turnips, plus onions or garlic OR intensive salad and leaf production: lettuce, spring onions, radishes, spinach, chard, Chinese greens

• Squashes and marrows are heavy feeders and will benefit most from manure.
• Sweetcorn will benefit from a dressing of high-nitrogen fertilizer.
• When early crops (eg broad beans) are harvested, sow late lettuce and other salad crops to take advantage of the nitrogen left behind by the legumes.
• If potatoes or members of the onion family are grown, ensure that three full seasons elapse before they are replanted in the same bed.

◄ A container overflowing with heliotropes contributes not only gorgeous purple, lavender and white hues, but also a mouth-watering vanilla fragrance. Though tender, heliotropes are easy to overwinter, frost-free, as rooted cuttings.

Groundwork: The area you have available for the permanent, structural planting will dictate how many beds you are able to lay out. For successful food production, each bed should be at least 2m (6ft) square, inside the hedge, to allow the crops room to develop. If you have the space, 3m (10ft) is even better. Pathways less than 60cm (2ft) wide become difficult to walk along; if too narrow, they will not look attractive and will create less dramatic vistas. Better, therefore, to go for the simplest pattern – even down to a single square, if that is all you have room for.

The easiest sequence of work is as follows:

1. Measure, lay out and pave the pathways.

2. Plant the box hedging, allowing 20–30cm (8–12in) between individual plants. Dig a roomy planting trench and be sure to plant into well-dug, healthy soil. Allow 15cm (6in) of space between the box plants and the edge of the paving, otherwise the hedge will overhang the path by too much.

3. Prepare the growing plots within the hedge boundaries, digging deeply and incorporating organic material to improve the soil. Seed for root crops can be sown directly into the ground. Sweetcorn, brassicas and members of the marrow family are best raised in containers, then planted out.

Potatoes are an excellent first crop, since they help to condition the soil. They also mature early, being harvested from midsummer to early autumn, and allow plenty of time for further treatment. Sweetcorn, being wind-pollinated, needs to grow in a single block. But if you want to enhance the beauty of the garden, most other crops can be 'mixed and matched', provided you adhere to the rules of crop rotation. Feathery carrot foliage, for example, makes a

❧ Lavender flowers are sweetly fragrant but must be picked when newly opened if they are to be dried for later use. Compact varieties like *L. angustifolia* 'Twickel Purple' are best for hedging.

Sweet corn is wind-pollinated and therefore develops the most uniform cobs if planted in blocks rather than rows.

❧ The flowers, as well as the leaves, of chives are edible and make decorative additions to green salads. This is a pink-flowered variety, *Allium schoenoprasum* 'Forescate'.

A wild species of tobacco plant (*Nicotiana langsdorffii*) whose lime-green flowers are shaped like flared bells and whose stamens are, uniquely, pale blue. These plants are in fact poisonous.

The darkest colours of agapanthus come from the species *A. inapertus*, whose flowers in the wild are a deep midnight blue. Barely frost-hardy, these plants can be overwintered under glass.

happy contrast with the glaucous leaves of cabbage, and red orach makes a colourful background to mixed ornamental brassicas.

Legumes – members of the pea and bean family – are unique in their ability to utilize free nitrogen, and therefore enrich the soil. It makes a lot of sense to follow them with such hungry feeders as courgettes, marrows or members of the cabbage family.

Maintenance: Kitchen gardens have a dynamism all their own. Unlike more peaceful flower or shrub borders, there will be a constant traffic here of harvest and replacement. The demands made on the soil in kitchen gardens are extreme. As crops are taken out, nutrients become depleted and need topping up. Make sure you have seedlings coming on for replacement and some speedy crops – lettuce, radishes and so on – to fill temporary gaps. For colour, do

not be afraid to pop in a few annuals or a herb or two grown for its pretty foliage. Make the most of the space by planting herbs along the edges of beds and consider containers of mint, strawberries or short-term herbs such as coriander or basil.

Box hedges will take a few years to develop. Once they are close to the desired height and shape, begin the annual clip, allowing the hedge to grow to the shape and dimensions you require.

Future: As long as the soil is properly treated, and if you are lucky enough to avoid disease problems, food production can go on for decades on the same area of ground. Watch out for weeds, particularly perennial kinds, and get rid of them immediately they appear. If disease does strike, be prepared to drop affected plants from your cropping plan for several years.

▼ Walls which face the sun are doubly valuable in a potager. As well as supplying support for wall plants, they help to protect the whole area from the worst of the weather. Here, young apples are ripening against the mellow brickwork.

❧ Because we eat them, rather than use them for ornament, the extraordinary textures and shapes of members of the cabbage family often pass us by. This is an ornamental kale whose thick leaves resemble elephant hide.

PLANT DIRECTORY

❧ *Allium schoenoprasum*
Chives. Neatly decorative, especially for bordering vegetable plots, these perennials develop thick tussocks of deep green leaves which are tubular and narrow, seldom exceeding 30cm (12in) in height. The bright purple-mauve blooms appear like little drumsticks in early summer and, like the leaves, can be plucked and eaten. The variety 'Forescate' has rich pink blooms and grows somewhat larger than common chives.

❧ *Brassicas, ornamental*
These biennial plants jump in and out of fashion about as frequently as shoulder pads. There are various forms, including kales and cabbages, all raised from the species *Brassica oleracea*. In the 'Osaka' cabbage series, the evergreen leaves are suffused with cream, pink or red hues. In winter, their colour intensifies, enabling these plants to present a dramatic display. The cabbages form open hearts, looking like huge roses. Ornamental kales – 'Northern Lights' is an example – have a more open habit, with leaves arranged along a lengthening stem.

❧ *Buxus sempervirens*
Box. The most popular hedging species is *B. sempervirens*; if you seek a dwarf form, try 'Suffruticosa'. Other species, useful for making a darker green contrast, include *B. balearica*, whose leaves are more blue-green than those of common box, and the diminutive *B microphylla*. These plants will grow into small or medium-sized trees, but are easily kept to tiny dimensions by a single annual clip.

❧ *Lathyrus odoratus*
Sweet peas. Annual climbers, whose branched, twining stems carrying pairs of glaucous green leaves and large, sweetly fragrant 'pea-flower' blooms. New varieties are constantly emerging but you should select for fragrance, above all else. Keep picking the flowers or dead-head assiduously to prolong the flowering season. Once they have been allowed to set seed, the plants will cease blooming.

❧ *Lavandula angustifolia*
Lavender. Beloved by the ancient Romans – who used it instead of shower gel – this fragrant Mediterranean shrub still retains universal appeal with its aromatic foliage and strongly scented blooms in purple, blue or pink. Compact varieties include 'Hidcote', whose flowers are dark blue, 'Twickel Purple' and 'Loddon Pink'. Fine for low hedges or for freestanding shrubs. Prune after flowering to retain compactness.

❧ *Rosmarinus officinalis*
Related to the lavenders, rosemary is useful for hedges, or free-growing as a small shrub. The narrow leaves, dark green with a pale grey underside, are intensely aromatic, with a gingery fragrance. The blue or blue-grey flowers produced in spring are irresistible to early bees.

RED-HOT BORDER

◄ The 'Domino' series of *Nicotiana x sanderae* comes in several shades including salmon-pink, white and this deep red. The flowering season lasts all through summer and, unlike those of some nicotianas, the flowers do not droop by day; their only drawback is that they lack the characteristic rich evening fragrance.

Of all borders designed in a particular colour scheme, red is possibly the most effective. Given full light, and preferably some strong sunshine, the red of some flowers is so intense that they seem almost to pulsate with energy as you stare at them. Even sombre reds glow with an inner warmth, but the scarlets dazzle – especially when suffused with orange – and if set to contrast with yellow flowers, they will give an almost physical buzz of energy. And as red is the complement of green, the leaves of your plants will never look more intensely green than when surrounded by red flowers.

◄ When planting for colour, it is often the background that gives the display its strength, rather than the colour itself. The power of this red border lies not just in the hue of the flowers, but in the way they have been juxtaposed with dark purplish foliage.

▼ Compared with the clean scarlet of verbenas and the other flowers that surround it, this prince's feather, *Amaranthus cruentus*, has suffusions of more sombre red, not only in the flowers but also in the maturing leaves.

Amaranthus, ornamental beet and dark canna foliage have been used together with sombre, fleshy-leaved sedums to create a heavy, brooding background among which the brilliance of the red flowers can shine out. This is strictly a summer display, long-lasting but not permanent because it is based largely on tender perennials such as dahlias and petunias.

At the height of the growing season it should be easy to develop a long-running display of vivid colour, but in winter and spring red is at a premium. Far from being a disadvantage, however, sporadic bursts of colour will make as much impact in the quiet seasons as a whole bed of red flowers in high summer. Consider carrying the red theme through spring with red wallflowers, or imagine a drift of scarlet anemones or a scattering of bright red tulips, such as the gorgeously bloody 'Couleur Cardinal', among the emerging perennials.

Ingredients

Key	Plant	Qty/Space (cm)	Substitute
①	*Amaranthus cruentus*	>3 /45	*Bassia scoparia*
②	*Berberis thunbergii* 'Atropurpurea'	1 /200	*Cotinus* 'Grace'
③	*Beta vulgaris* 'McGregor's Favourite'	>3 /45	*B. v.* 'Iresine'
④	*Canna indica* 'Roi Humbert'	3 /100	*Rosa* 'Rote Max Graf'
⑤	*Crocosmia* 'Lucifer'	3 /100	*Lobelia tupa*
⑥	*Dahlia*, assorted red	>5 /60	*Lobelia cardinalis*
⑦	*Nicotiana* 'Domino Crimson'	>10 /30	*Salvia x superba*
⑧	*Petunia* (any red series)	>5 /30	*Pelargonium* (any red series)
⑨	*Penstemon* 'Firebird'	>5 /45	*P. hartwegii*
⑩	*Rosa glauca*	1 /200	*Corylus avellana* 'Fuscorubra'
⑪	*Sedum telephium* ssp. *maximum* 'Atropurpureum'	>10 /60	*Knautia macedonica*

Qty: *the number of specimens used in this recipe; numbers can be adjusted to suit a different site.*
Space: *recommended spacings for optimum growth (in centimetres).*

The succulent foliage of *Sedum telephium* adds an extra texture to this border and the deep, brooding purple of the variety 'Atropurpureum' makes it an ideal candidate for inclusion in a red border.

Planting Plan   3.5m x 2.5m (12ft x 8ft)

Groundwork: Frequent replanting and fast-growing summer flowers call for good, rich soil which has been dug thoroughly and dressed generously with fertilizer or manure.
Planting procedure: This planting needs careful planning. The permanent outline or framework plants are the big shrubs — *Rosa glauca* and the berberis — and they should be planted 2–3m (6–10ft) apart at the back of the border. Position cannas and crocosmia roughly 1m (3ft) in front of these.

The rest of the planting must be planned as a pattern, but avoid a regular repetition of shapes, unless you want a formalized bedding display. Mark out chosen areas and plant nicotianas, penstemons, petunias and dahlias in bold groups. Follow the suggestions in the plant list for individual spacings, but keep your groups of strong colours as discreet as possible. Try to tier the planting, with shorter subjects in front of taller ones. Make sure there is enough space between the groups,

Two long-lasting herbaceous plants, continually in bloom and, if well fed, constantly fresh-looking, are *Verbena* x *hybrida* and large-flowered petunias. Though technically perennials, they are usually grown as annuals.

The Indian shot plant (*Canna indica*) is a vigorous perennial which, though happy in any fertile soil, relishes moisture and a warm climate. 'Roi Humbert', above, has deep purple foliage as well as a long run of red blooms.

The red colour in hybrid penstemons comes from the American species, *P. hartwegii*. Though vigorous and easy to grow, few of them are reliably frost-hardy.

▼ Dark foliage, in this case from dahlias and *Sedum telephium*, helps to heighten the drama of the red flowers. On their own, the flowers would have less impact.

since this is where you will be placing the dark-leaved temporary 'filler' plants – the sedum, amaranthus and ornamental beet. Your aim is to create strong islands of bright red in a dark sea.

Maintenance: Interim feeding, especially on thin, light soils, will ensure constant flowering. Good weed control is crucial in a planting of such close harmony, since any plant of the wrong character will stand out unhappily. Keep dead-heading dahlias and penstemons, to ensure a constant run of fresh flowers. If gaps appear, be ready to add new plants, either dark-leaved or good strong red annuals or tender perennials, to fill them.

Many of these plants are tender and so the first autumn frost could ruin the border and destroy much of your stock. Be sure to take cuttings during summer and overwinter the resulting young plants under glass for use in future years. Plants left in the ground must be protected from frost.

PLANT DIRECTORY

❧ *Amaranthus cruentus*
Purple amaranth. Coarse, somewhat hairy annuals with large, broad leaves, often bronze or purplish in colour, and tufted masses of tiny maroon or red flowers which appear like large tassels from mid-summer onwards. In many varieties, the seedheads are as attractive as the flowers.

❧ *Beta vulgaris*
Ornamental beet. Relatives of the sugar beet and spinach, but with decorative foliage and stems. Technically, these are biennials and will die once they have set seed, but some kinds will resist bolting for most of the season. 'McGregor's Favourite' has dark purple foliage; 'Vulcan' is similar but less dark in hue. A lovely edible alternative is simply the red form of rhubarb chard or Swiss chard. Sow seed in spring each year.

❧ *Canna indica*
Indian shot plant. Erect-growing perennials which, in moist conditions, will exceed 1.75m (5ft) in height. Their thick, fleshy stems are furnished with broad oval leaves, often dark bronze or vivid green. The flowers have their parts arranged in threes, a little like irises; in warm areas they are produced in constant succession all through summer. Their colours are mostly hot and strong – red, orange, scarlet and yellow.

❧ *Crocosmia*
Corm-bearing South African perennials with brash sheaves of vivid green sword-like leaves. In mid- to late summer, the flower stems emerge and soon develop dainty side-stems which carry bell-shaped flowers whose petals curve outwards. Colours are always warm, ranging through yellow and orange to bright red.

❧ *Petunia*
Possibly the world's most popular summer bedding plant. A South American genus whose somewhat glutinous stems and limp foliage are furnished, for the entire growing season, with trumpet-shaped blooms in almost every colour imaginable – even yellow! Good varieties are introduced constantly, but an interesting recent trend has been the development of such trailing varieties as 'Surfinia' and the small-flowered 'Million Bells'.

FOCUS ON FOLIAGE

► *Melianthus major* sports the coolest of blue-green leaf colours, especially when grown in fertile soil in full sun. The large, exquisitely beautiful serrated leaves make a good foil for flowering plants.

◄ The common name 'red-hot poker' can be misleading with such varieties as *Kniphofia* 'Little Maid', whose soft, greenish-cream flowers help to sustain a cool effect. Unlike many kniphofias, this one is a tidy, compact grower, seldom exceeding 60cm (2ft) tall. Its long flowering period sometimes lasts from midsummer to autumn.

A luscious blend of foliage chosen for its contrasting textures and colours gives this summer planting an air of fresh exuberance. In an intriguing reversal, much of the colour comes from the foliage, whereas a significant proportion of the flowers are green or greenish. Silver, purple-bronze and blue-grey leaf tones highlight the display, backed by discreet flashes of vivid flower colour and made more dramatic by placing large, felty leaves next to soft, feathery foliage.

A planting like this can be adapted to suit a bed of any size. The photograph shows a small part of a larger border, less than 2.5m (8ft) long and stretching back no more than that. But this joyous mix of foliage and flower could be bulked up to fill a larger border or scaled down even further to develop a modest corner, or even a little gap between walls or buildings. Such big, bold foliage is hard to sustain for the whole of the summer – what we see here is a climax of growth, rather than a steady run – but the planting includes species such as *Verbena* 'Sissinghurst' and dahlias, which will work hard to extend the season. The form and foliage of melianthus, the artemisia in the foreground and the irises will give sustained interest with their grey-green leaves, and the flowers of several plants will add colour from early summer into mid-autumn. The seasonal climax is enhanced here by using a high proportion of tender summer material such as nicotianas, verbena, *Salvia argentea* and the lovely leafy *Melianthus major*, much of which will need to be replaced with bulbs and early flowers for winter and spring.

◄ Rich leaf colours with dramatic contrasts of texture form the basis of this planting, with the feathery tufts of *Artemisia schmidtiana* and the big felty leaves of *Salvia argentea* striking a silver note to ring against the more sombre purple foliage of the dahlia. Irises add a further variation with their spiky leaves. The unique blue-grey foliage of *Melianthus major* is just beginning to peep above the tobacco flowers at the back of the border; it will make a full contribution later in the season. The purple blooms of meadow rue give an airy display at the border back. Though not especially long-lived in flower, the persistent foliage of this plant is ferny and delicate.

Planting Plan   2.5m x 2.5m (8ft x 8ft)

Ingredients

Key Plant	Qty/Space (cm)	Substitute
① Artemisia schmidtiana	5 /25	A. pedemontana, A. pontica
② Dahlia 'Preston Park'	3 /75	D. 'Bishop of Llandaff'
③ Eryngium alpinum	1 /60	E. giganteum
④ Kniphofia 'Little Maid'	1 /60	K. 'Green Jade'
⑤ Melianthus major	1 /90	Romneya coulteri
⑥ Nicotiana 'Lime Green'	5 /30	N. affinis
⑦ Rosa officinalis	1 /150	R. 'Tuscany'
⑧ Salvia argentea	3 /30	Stachys olympica
⑨ Thalictrum delavayi 'Hewitt's Double'	3 /75	Campanula lactiflora 'Loddon Anna'
⑩ Verbena 'Sissinghurst'	3 /30	Pelargonium 'Paton's Unique'

Replacements for Summer Plants
Numbers correspond to those for original plants

② Erysimum cheiri 'Vulcan'	10 /30	Any purple or red wallflower
⑥ Tulipa 'Spring Green'	30 /20	T. purissima – or mix the two
⑧ Crocus 'Jeanne d'Arc'	20 /10	Muscari botryoides 'Alba'

Qty: *the number of specimens used in this recipe; numbers can be adjusted to suit a different site.*
Space: *recommended spacings for optimum growth (in centimetres).*

Salvia argentea is more valuable for its softly puckered, pale grey, felty foliage than for the sprays of white, hook-shaped flowers which appear later in midsummer.

Dahlia 'Preston Park', a medium-height variety, has the double attributes of vivid red, single flowers whose chocolate centres are dusted with orange pollen, and lustrous, purple-bronze leaves.

Groundwork: Plants in this luxuriant recipe are hungry feeders, benefiting from rich, well-watered soil. Such summer specials as nicotianas and dahlias respond particularly well to feeding and mulching, since they have so much growing to do in a relatively short season. Whenever plants are removed, or replaced, be sure to work extra compost plus a little slow-release fertilizer – bonemeal is good or you could use blood, fish and bonemeal – into the soil to keep the level of fertility high.

As long as there is plenty of light, most of the plants will stand up well enough without support, but be prepared to use pea sticks or linking stakes for support, especially if your garden is exposed, or if lower light levels draw the plants up.

Planting procedure: In this mixed border, where permanent and temporary (tender) plants are growing in association, you will need to replant at least twice each year. Begin by assembling the permanent species: kniphofia, eryngium, thalictrum and the shrub rose. In dry areas, the silver plants may well survive the winter, but it is safest to plant them in spring, when the soil is warming up. The artemisia is small and slow-growing, so plant a tight group no more than 15cm (6in) apart if you want a speedy

◀ The combination of bright scarlet dahlia flowers and wine-pink verbenas is surprising. The dahlia's purple foliage makes an effective link between the colours, complementing both but also helping to separate the two.

🐾 *Kniphofia* 'Little Maid' is one of several pokers with flowers in cool, soft colours. 'Green Jade' is similar but taller and 'Toffee Nosed' has flowers which open caramel-coloured and fade to cream.

🐾 Green flowers are always intriguing, perhaps because the colour is unexpected. *Nicotiana* 'Lime Green' provides a run of bloom all summer.

🐾 The evergreen, feathery foliage of *Artemisia schmidtiana* creates a filigree effect, perfect for contrasting with more solid leaves. Although the flowers are insignificant, few plants have such silvery leaves.

PLANT DIRECTORY

🐾 *Artemisia*
Wormwood. A large, mainly Mediterranean genus of herbs and shrubs grown almost exclusively for their finely divided, filigree foliage. Leaf colour varies from dull grey-green to an almost pure, silvery white. Plant size varies too, from the low-growing *A. schmidtiana* at 15cm (6in) to the taller, shrubbier *A. absinthium* which can reach 90cm (3ft). Best in full sun, on a free-draining soil. Drought-tolerant.

🐾 *Kniphofia*
Red-hot poker. South African natives belonging to the lily family with narrow, somewhat coarse, grassy foliage and vivid foxtail flowers. They have hybridized with ease, producing varieties in a full range of hues from soft cream, through yellows and oranges to scarlet. Excellent for architectural planting, but untidy unless sited carefully.

🐾 *Melianthus major*
A very distinctive plant from Africa, grown for the beauty of its huge toothed, pinnate leaves which are a striking glaucous grey-green. The clustered, rusty-brown flowers, when they emerge, are not especially exciting. Its ultimate height can be as much as 2.7m (9ft) but, since this plant is not frost-hardy, it is usually planted out in cold areas and therefore seldom reaches full maturity. Propagate from cuttings or offshoots.

🐾 *Nicotiana*
Tobacco. Popular as bedding plants but also having great character for less formal plantings. Lovely species include *N. sylvestris*, a tall-growing plant with pendulous white blooms, and *N. langsdorffii*, whose small, cupped blooms are lime-green, each with a central tuft of smoky-blue stamens. The best modern seed series include 'Domino' in green, maroon and salmon-pink hues. Various heights. None is frost-hardy.

🐾 *Thalictrum*
Meadow rue. Members of the buttercup family, usually with very finely divided, lacy or ferny foliage and often with big sprays of frail, ephemeral flowers which give a misty effect. Most decorative is the purple-bloomed *T. delavayi*, especially 'Hewitt's Double' which sports twice the number of petals and therefore makes twice the impact. Other good garden meadow rues include yellow-flowered *T. flavum* and the low-growing maidenhair-like *T. minus*.

🐾 *Verbena*
A precious genus bearing jewel-like flowers, often for the entire growing season. *V.* 'Sissinghurst' is one of the most dependably perennial forms, with a trailing habit, lobed or cut leaves and long-lasting umbels of wine-pink flowers. Stems take root wherever they come into contact with the ground, making this plant easy to propagate and excellent at forming generous mats of colour. Not frost-hardy. Propagate from cuttings or small rooted divisions.

spread. The remaining temporary plants — verbena, salvia, nicotiana, melianthus and the dahlia — should not be planted out until all risk of frost has passed. Make sure they are spaced far enough from the perennials to avoid overcrowding. You may need to thin plants out, or remove parts of them so that everything has room to flourish but without encroaching on a neighbour.

Maintenance: Once the summer planting is established, it should be largely self-maintaining. Picking over to remove dead leaves or blooms helps with the overall appearance of the planting, and you will need to keep an eye open for signs of disease. Remove kniphofia flowers before they set seed — to encourage plants to produce more flower spikes — and cut the artemisia flowers back to stimulate the production of more foliage.

AN ARID PLANTING

Despite the brashness of the tones, this arrangement pays more than mere lip service to art. The structure or bones of the garden are strong and durable, using tall trees to frame the building and bold structural plants – agave, opuntia and a Canary Island echium – to give the lower levels a strong outline.

The understorey planting is rich with hot colours – vivid purple from the South American verbena, sharp orange from the

▶ Californian poppies (*Eschscholzia californica*) have become popular drought-resistant plants throughout the temperate world. The wild species is orange or golden-yellow, but garden forms include a range of hues from pale cream through salmon to bright pink.

In a frost-free climate, where brilliant sunshine is the norm and where rain falls sparingly – mostly in winter – you can afford to be daring with colours, since the brightest hues are needed to show up in strong light. Hot orange, brilliant yellow and loud purple come together in this subtropical garden to provide a warm, welcoming display, amply set off by lush foliage in silvery grey or deep green. To achieve a similar effect in a cool climate you would have to use temporary tender species.

▶ In this subtropical garden an exciting blend of foliage and flower provides a rich mix of contrasting colours and textures. Succulents hint at the dryness of the climate, but the garden's display of luxuriant foliage and its wealth of flowers demonstrate how, with thoughtful selection, it is possible to create a feeling of lushness even in an arid spot. The stark whiteness of the building makes a delightful foil for the dark leaves of the shading trees. The dense planting in the foreground reinforces the wonderful sense of extravagance.

Californian poppies and a bright patch from the silver-leaved, white-flowered cerastium. But these noisy hues are cushioned by plenty of lush foliage, particularly from the silvery salvia in the foreground and by a denser planting of greenery in the shade of the tall trees. Extra fillips come from the sea lavender (*Limonium perezii*) and from the glowing red flowers of the New Zealand tea tree (*Leptospermum scoparium*).

The delight of growing a Mediterranean-style garden in a frost-free climate is that the choice of plants is almost unlimited. In a cold climate you must be a bit more circumspect, but there is still a huge range of easy plants that are both drought-resistant and beautiful. Furthermore, long summer days can enable subtropical plants not only to survive outdoors but also to grow at an astonishing rate, thus establishing themselves within a single season.

▲ The prickly pear (*Opuntia* species) has water-storing stems which are flattened and rounded, creating an unmistakable outline. In a cold climate, these plants would need to be overwintered in a frost-free place, but in a warm garden they can grow to several metres high and across. The spines on some species are highly irritant.

Ingredients

Key	Plant	Qty/Space (cm)	Substitute
①	Agave americana	1 /300	Cordyline australis
②	Arctotis fastuosa	5 /45	Gaillardia × grandiflora
③	Beaucarnea recurvata	3 /60	Kniphofia caulescens
④	Cerastium tomentosum	5 /20	Artemisia ludoviciana
⑤	Diascia barbarae	3 /20	Dianthus deltoides
⑥	Echium fastuosum	1 /200	Buddleja 'Lochinch'
⑦	Eschscholzia californica	seed	Papaver 'Shirley Series'
⑧	Kalanchoe beharenis	1 /30	
⑨	Leptospermum scoparium	1 /200	Indigofera amblyantha
⑩	Limonium perezii	1 /60	Crambe maritima
⑪	Opuntia robusta	1 /300	Colletia paradoxa
⑫	Rosmarinus officinalis	1 /100	Phlomis fruticosa
⑬	Salvia clevlandii	1 /100	Dorycnium hirsutum
⑭	Tagetes lemmonii	1 /100	Grindelia chiloensis
⑮	Verbena peruviana	5 /30	Geranium dalmaticum

Qty: the number of specimens used in this recipe; numbers can be adjusted to suit a different site.
Space: recommended spacings for optimum growth (in centimetres).

🍃 In a hot, dry garden, white makes a cooling contrast. Snow-on-the-mountain (Cerastium tomentosum) flowers in early summer, with thousands of small white blooms. The low mats of pale silver-grey foliage create a soft, cool effect.

🍃 Plants with sword-like leaves can be used to make strong architectural statements. Here a century plant (Agave americana), with its armed, fleshy leaves creates a dramatic focal point.

Planting Plan   10m x 15m (33ft x 50ft)

✓ The New Zealand tea tree (*Leptospermum scoparium*) is a beautiful member of the myrtle family with conifer-like foliage. Its small, brightly coloured blossoms last for months.

From the Canary Islands and Madeira come a number of *Echium* species which grow into robust shrubs smothered in gorgeous, translucent blue or pinkish flower spikes.

One of the most common of the Mediterranean aromatic shrubs, rosemary is useful as a flavoursome herb and a shapely ornamental. The pale blue flowers are sweetly fragrant.

✓ Sea lavenders (*Limonium*) are surprisingly drought-tolerant and flower for many weeks during summer. The papery flowers, small and white, are borne on brilliant purple stems and calyces, making the plants colourful even after the last true petals have fallen.

Groundwork: Water conservation is essential, even for drought-tolerant plants. Check that drainage is adequate and dress the ground with mulches, to reduce evaporation and to ensure as little bare earth as possible. A thick cover of plants will help conserve moisture and keep the soil in good condition.

Feeding should be modest – just enough to overcome any mineral deficiencies but not so much that the plants grow soft and lush. A very light general dressing, of either rotted manure or organic general fertilizer in early spring, will suffice for most of the plants. Larger shrubs, especially those which are regularly pruned, will benefit from an application of bonemeal in spring.

Planting procedure: First, mark out positions for the main architectural plants. The succulents and the echium flank the statue in this garden, emphasizing that the structure here comes as much from the plants as from artefacts. Place your key plants so that they are comfortable with the positions of surrounding objects – the house, garage and existing large trees. Understorey plants need careful positioning too. Most are in discrete groups, touching at their edges, but seldom merging into one another. Space your plants evenly within the groups, but in asymmetric shapes overall, to avoid unnatural-looking blocks. The eschscholzias have spread themselves around with little inhibition and although this can be encouraged, you may want to remove a proportion of seed capsules to avoid an overabundance of seedlings.

It should be easy to achieve continuity through the summer, since the majority of these plants have a long flowering period. Bulbs will contribute intense but temporary displays in spring, without hogging too much space. Mediterranean species of anemone, iris and fritillary and the lovely South African ixia, gladiolus or nerine all benefit from a fierce summer baking which will ripen their bulbs and ensure good blooms.

Maintenance: Once the plant cover is well established, maintenance is simple. The mulch will help to reduce weeds but be vigilant about unwelcome plants that pop up. Repeat-flowering perennials are always better for being dead-headed from time to time; if given a gentle feed after being trimmed back, they will often grow with renewed vigour. A general tidy-up will be needed in winter.

PLANT DIRECTORY

✓ *Agave americana*
Century plant. A New World succulent whose fleshy rosettes may exceed 2m (6ft) in height and width. The fiercely armed, sword-shaped leaves, each ending in a sharp thorn, may be plain thyme-green or variegated. The juice is highly irritant, but the leaf fibres have, for centuries, been used to make sisal string. After a number of years, especially if the plant is under stress, a huge inflorescence develops, flowering at more than 6m (20ft), after which the plant dies. It is barely frost-hardy.

✓ *Cerastium tomentosum*
Snow-on-the-mountain. An invasive but charming perennial in the pink and carnation family, with silver, slightly downy simple leaves on trailing stems. In early summer the plants are covered with creamy-white, single flowers. They grow to only 15cm (6in) high, but a single plant will spread up to 1m (3ft) across in time.

✓ *Leptospermum scoparium*
New Zealand tea tree. A shrub, rather than a tree, but able to grow as high as 3m (10ft) in good conditions. Its graceful, arching stems are covered with small, pointed leaves and, in spring and early summer, with masses of tiny, five-petalled flowers. In the wild, these are always white or pale pink, but cultivars range through stronger pinks, in such varieties as 'Kiwi', to the dark-leaved, deep red-flowered 'Red Damask'.

✓ *Limonium latifolium*
Sea lavender. A number of species are especially decorative. From the warm-climate Macaronesian island of Madeira and the Canaries, such species as *L. perezii*, *L. arborescens* and *L. fruticans* actually grow into low shrubs, always with long-lasting, purple-blue inflorescences. More widely grown in gardens, the annual *L. latifolium* (statice) is as lovely in its true wild form as in such selected clones as the darker purple 'Violetta'. They are popular as everlasting flowers since their papery bracts retain their colour even after they have been desiccated.

✓ *Opuntia*
Prickly pear. A Central and South American genus of ungainly plants, whose thorny stems are flattened and oval. Some species grow tall – up to 3m (10ft). *O. robusta* carries yellow flowers in late spring, followed later by fruits that turn reddish as they ripen; these are edible. Not frost-hardy.

✓ *Verbena peruviana*
Tender perennials of immense value, not only because of their vigour, when grown in the sun, but also because they are seldom out of flower. This species has deeply divided foliage and rich magenta flowers. It is easy to propagate, either by division or from cuttings, or – easier still – you can simply rip chunks of the plant out of the ground and replant the torn-off pieces!

A SHADY
URBAN OASIS

▶ A rich mixture of shapes and textures guarantees constant interest in this shaded corner. The dark green, palmate leaves of the hellebore stand out strongly against a softer background. In the foreground, astilbes blend with other ground-cover plants, adding a tiny touch of colour with their pinkish-white flowers.

A dashing plant selection, with a strong emphasis on fresh, green foliage, has transformed this gloomy back garden into a plant enthusiast's paradise. Not only have shade-loving species been chosen, but a number have white or pale-coloured flowers, ensuring that they stand out in the low light levels. The garden is interesting in all seasons, with a large proportion of evergreens for winter interest, hellebores and bergenia whose blooms connect winter to spring, and a selection of climbers with flowers that decorate the overhanging foliage in summer.

◄ Ferns provide their own special effects, always looking fresh with their unfurling fronds. The soft shield fern (*Polystichum setiferum*) is doubly valuable, being evergreen, totally hardy and able to tolerate considerable drought provided it is not in direct sun.

Town gardens tend to be narrow, often with high fences, walls or buildings casting more shade than is ideal and preventing enough rainfall watering the soil. This can result in the most challenging of sites: dry shade. Getting plants established may be difficult in such conditions and colour will always be at a premium. But with careful plant selection, and a good deal of trial and error, it is

perfectly possible to develop a magnificent garden whose interest is sustained throughout the entire year.

This garden has a strong framework, consisting of high walls furnished with climbing and wall plants, with ornamental shrubs set in front of them. The initial impression is one of overall greenery but there are flowering trees, conifers, climbers

and broad-leaved, glossy evergreens all working together to compose the varied and interesting outline. Within this plant framework, individual features are minimal but nevertheless strong. A path and steps lead to a mysterious door behind which lies the street. Imagine the joy of opening the doorway from a hard concrete pavement and entering this cool oasis of green delights.

◄ There is just enough bloom in this planting to attract attention, but the main focus is definitely the foliage. Every imaginable shape and surface texture is evident here, with an interesting range of leaf colours too. Notice how sparingly variegated foliage has been used – no more than a patch of cream-margined ivy, a golden grass and the natural leaf markings of the lungwort. All other colour variety comes from gradations of green. The scarcity of flower helps to enhance this green symphony, but the blooms that are there show great class. Among the most intriguing are the saxifrages in the foreground, a beautiful white gentian, the strangely pungent *Clerodendrum trichotomum* and, as a centrepoint by the gate, a dazzling white hydrangea.

Among plants which grow happily in moist, peaty soil in shade or semi-shade, the smaller astilbes – particularly *Astilbe simplicifolia* – are especially suitable.

The mind-your-own-business plant (*Soleirolia soleirolii*) is an effective ground-cover plant for shade, but in the wrong place it can become an invasive nuisance.

🍂 Unhappily named the stinking hellebore – though its pungency is not unpleasant – *Helleborus foetidus* is one of the most valuable hardy winter plants. This form is Wester Flisk Group.

Shrubs with creamy-white flowers, like this *Hydrangea arborescens* 'Grandiflora', show up especially well in shade. The colour comes from sterile florets; the true flowers are tiny.

Planting Plan 3m x 7m (10ft x 23ft)

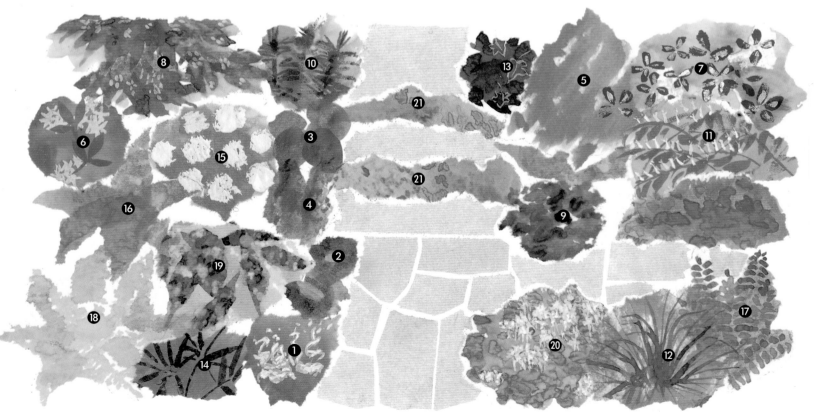

Plants that have beautiful flowers as well as characterful foliage are precious. This lungwort, *Pulmonaria saccharata*, is evergreen but has pink and blue flowers in spring.

A golden grass with a graceful, flowing character, *Hakonechloa macra* 'Aureola' is happy either in a container or in open ground.

Ingredients

Key	Plant	Qty/Space (cm)	Substitute
1	Astilbe simplicifolia 'Alba'	1 /45	A. 'Sprite'
2	Bergenia ciliata	1 /45	B. purpurascens
3	Bergenia cordifolia	1 /60	B. crassifolia
4	Campanula trachelium	1 /45	C. persicifolia
5	Chamaecyparis lawsoniana	1 /300	Any medium conifer
6	Choisya ternata	1 /120	C. 'Aztec Pearl'
7	Clematis 'Etoile Rose'	1 /100	C. 'Minuet'
8	Clerodendrum trichotomum	1 /180	Eucryphia 'Nymansay'
9	Duchesne indica	>3 /15	Persicaria vaccinifolia
10	Euphorbia characias	1 /120	E. mellifera
11	Gentiana asclepiadea var. alba	1 /45	Polygonatum odoratum
12	Hakonechloa macra 'Aureola'	3 /30	Milium effusum 'Aureum'
13	Hedera helix 'Heise'	1 /120	H. h. 'Adam'
14	Helleborus foetidus 'Wester Flisk'	1 /90	H. argutifolius
15	Hydrangea arborescens 'Grandiflora'	1 /150	H. quercifolia
16	Onoclea sensibilis	1 /60	Blechnum tabulare
17	Osmunda regia	1 /100	Dryopteris erythrosora
18	Polystichum setiferum 'Plumosomultilobum'	1 /90	Athyrium niponicum var. pictum
19	Pulmonaria saccharata	1 /60	P. officinalis
20	Saxifraga fortunei	>3 /45	S. x urbium
21	Soleirolia soleirolii	>3 /20	Raoulia australis

Qty: the number of specimens used in this recipe; numbers can be adjusted to suit a different site.
Space: recommended spacings for optimum growth (in centimetres).

Groundwork: Every inch counts in this restricted space, so it is important that plants receive the best possible growing conditions. The soil must be in perfect heart and, since this is inclined to be a dry spot, care must be taken to minimize moisture loss. The plant cover itself will help, but thick mulches will ensure better moisture retention.

Planting procedure: The outline plants will need a headstart on the rest, to avoid being swamped. If this planting is phased over two years, begin with the conifers, clerodendrum, choisya and other skeleton shrubs such as the hydrangea. The remainder is really infill and can be added as and when it suits you or your pocket. Ferns, hellebores and some of the crevice plants may take longer to establish than the rest, so could benefit from a little extra attention in their first season, watering if necessary, and preventing neighbours swamping them.

The trick, here, is to tread that fine line between dense planting and overcrowding. Do not be afraid of planting too densely at first – you may have to, to ensure a good early display – but be ready to thin the planting down as soon as it becomes necessary. Do not feel obliged to stick rigidly to the precise positioning here, but take in the planned juxtapositions: rounded contrasted with fussy foliage, coloured leaves against green and flowers against an uncluttered background. Add compost according to need.

It is often more difficult to coax plants into flowering in deep shade than in full light, and when they do bloom, their colours are not as rich as they are in full sun. But most shade plants carry blooms in white or soft pastel shades and this is an advantage, since pale colours show up better in low light.

Maintenance: Remove leaves as they die or become damaged and be ready to plant replacements to fill any noticeable gaps.

Future: Small gardens become overgrown quickly, but they are easy to overhaul, either by rearranging all the plants or adjusting areas that are not quite working. Do not be afraid to try different plants: the best way to find out if a species will thrive in your garden conditions is to plant it and see.

PLANT DIRECTORY

Bergenia cordifolia
Tough enough to survive in its native Siberia, this perennial has broad, leathery evergreen leaves with a shiny surface, puckered and creased when young. In autumn, in hard weather, these are burnished with purplish bronze. The pink flowers start to open in late winter, down in the base of the plant, and continue, on lengthening stems, well into summer.

Choisya ternata
Mexican orange. An evergreen shrub with aromatic glossy leaves – each composed of three leaflets – and fragrant, waxy white flowers in spring and summer. It is capable of growing 2.5m (8ft) across but is better if pruned to shape from time to time. The flowers are sometimes spoilt by late frosts.

Clerodendrum trichotomum
A small, shapely tree whose branches tend to form natural tiers; it has large, dark green leaves and creamy-white spider-like flowers. The fruits, when they form, are a brilliant blue-black, making an exciting contrast with the calyces which become rosy-red as they ripen. The form 'Fargesii' has darker foliage, purple in bud, turning green as it matures.

Gentiana asclepiadea
Tallish herbaceous gentian from Asia Minor with willow-like foliage produced along arching 75cm (2ft 6in) long stems. The flowers, which develop both along the stems and at the tips, are dusky blue and tube-shaped, with five-rayed stars at their openings. The white form, *G. a.* var. *alba* is as lovely, but there is also a gorgeous hybrid, 'Knightshayes', whose dark blue flowers have white throats.

Helleborus foetidus
Stinking hellebore. A plant with an unfortunate common name, it is a striking, evergreen perennial, growing almost like a shrub to 60cm (2ft), with distinctive, very dark green palmate leaves, slightly toothed along their margins, and with a bitter, pungent smell when crushed. The small, cup-shaped flowers, which appear in late winter, are pale green, often with maroon or reddened edges to their sepals. They are borne on much branched, fleshy stems which are noticeably paler than the leaves. The plant is poisonous in all its parts.

Polystichum setiferum
Soft shield fern. One of the most drought-proof of the ferns, long cultivated in a wide number of garden forms. *P. s.* 'Plumosomultilobum' is even lovelier than the wild form, having extra divisions in its foliage and creating a softer, more feathery effect. These ferns are evergreen.

Saxifraga fortunei
Though it has the prettiest of the saxifrage flowers, this plant is grown chiefly for its handsome foliage. Rounded, toothed leaves about 8cm (3in) across are green above and purplish below, often with leaf markings. The autumn flowers, produced in loose panicles, are soft white, with short upper but long lower petals, giving an impression of dancing insects.

BY THE WATER'S EDGE

◄ Lysichiton, an invasive relative of the arum, occurs wild both in Asia and in the New World. *Lysichiton americanum* produces large yellow spathes in spring, followed in summer by huge leaves, sometimes more than 1m (3ft) long.

Waterside and wetland planting is distinctive. In wild landscapes, water levels alter so that, after rain or flood, marginal plants used to growing on relatively dry land may find their roots immersed whereas, during drought, they could be left high and dry for weeks. Happy in such changeable conditions, these plants can be used to create sumptuous summer displays along the margins of your water feature. Bog and waterside plants tend to be big and brassy, often with dramatic

Every garden, regardless of style or size, benefits from the inclusion of a water feature. Water has allure: all living things are attracted to it and, once your attention is caught, you can relax and allow the water to have its hypnotic effect. With its ability to reflect images from the surface, and to bounce daylight back so that it can illuminate dark corners or low-lying areas, water brings an extra dimension to the garden. A pond or a bog garden provides shelter and sustenance for wildlife, as well as presenting a whole range of new planting opportunities.

foliage or strong flower colour making their reflections doubly gorgeous.

Most wetland species have vigorous, often creeping root systems and grow into large clumps or mats which will readily merge to form an almost impenetrable barrier of vegetation at the waterside. Exceptions are the Asiatic primulas, whose seedlings are easily swamped but whose exquisite form and colour, in early summer, make them the most sought-after of wetland plants.

▲ Floating leaves are essential to maintain balance in a pond. By shading the water, they inhibit the growth of damaging algae such as blanketweed and, in summer, they help to prevent the water temperature from rising too high. This yellow-flowered water lily is *Nymphaea* 'Marliacea Chromatella'.

◀ This large garden pond in an informal setting has been planted with a rich collection of wetland plants, from hostas and Japanese candelabra primulas to European irises and American relatives of the arum. Although the first water lilies have yet to open, their foliage is already covering more than half the water surface – essential for a healthy pond in summer – and a rich floral display is clearly on the way. Bold, broad foliage, furnished here by hostas and ligularias, makes a strong contrast with the rigid, narrow leaves of the yellow flag irises, their upright habit emphasized by the gold and green stripes in their variegation.

Planting Plan   pond min: 8 sq m (25 sq ft)

Groundwork: Establishment can be a messy business, especially in natural bogs. These may be too wet to dig over and horrible to delve into with bare hands but, once your plants are established, they should grow densely enough to inhibit weed development. The conventional rules of digging holes, planting and firming plants in with your feet may have to be abandoned in very wet land. In such cases, disturb the ground as little as possible – it may be simply a matter of pushing roots down into the ooze!

Where the pond has been installed using a butyl liner, the surrounding soil will be less wet and conventional planting is possible. Be careful not to damage the liner as you work and, where marginals are to be planted in the water, use baskets or containers and place them on a marginal 'shelf' in the pool.

Planting procedure: Begin by siting the key or anchor plants: the variegated iris,

hostas, royal fern and the shrubs. Make sure you leave plenty of room for the Asiatic primulas: these may be raised from seed – or you can purchase young plants – and planted out in the autumn or early spring 30–45cm (12–18in) apart. In ideal conditions they will seed themselves but they usually have to be replaced from time to time. Collected seed should do as well as purchased seed: confine your collecting to the best plants. Submerged green plants are essential for providing oxygen to the water, and those with floating leaves will shade the water, preventing the excess development of algae.

Maintenance: Weeding can be tricky in a bog or waterside garden: avoid digging but pull up troublesome arrivals by hand. Prevent rampant characters – like the iris or ligularias – from invading the hostas or burying less vigorous species. Natural spreading will help to suppress weed development.

❧ Plants with a brief flowering season need good foliage to carry them through the quiet periods. This variegated form of yellow flag, *Iris pseudacorus*, looks handsome all summer.

❧ Like an outsize ragwort, *Ligularia dentata* produces generous sprays of bright golden to orange flowers above handsome rounded or heart-shaped leaves.

Ingredients

Key	Plant	Qty/Space (cm)	Substitute
①	Caltha palustris var. palustris	>5 /90	C. palustris
②	Hemerocallis lilioasphodelus	1 /60	Any day lily hybrid
③	Hosta sieboldiana	1 /75	H. 'Sum and Substance'
④	Hosta tokudama	1 /75	H. 'Frances Williams'
⑤	Iris pseudacorus	1 /60	I. kaempferi
⑥	Iris pseudacorus 'Variegata'	>10 /60	I. laevigata
⑦	Iris sibirica	3 /45	I. chrysographes
⑧	Ligularia dentata 'Desdemona'	3 /90	L. d. 'Orange Princess'
⑨	Ligularia glabrescens	1 /90	L. przewalskii
⑩	Lysichiton americanum	1 /90	Symplocarpus foetidus
⑪	Nectaroscordum siculum bulgaricum	>3 /30	Allium giganteum
⑫	Nymphaea 'Marliacea Chromatella'	To suit size of pond (see Directory)	
⑬	Osmunda regalis	3 /90	Aruncus dioicus
⑭	Primula bulleyana	>5 /45	P. prolifera
⑮	Primula florindae	3 /45	P. sikkimensis
⑯	Primula pulverulenta	>5 /45	P. japonica
⑰	Ranunculus aconitifolius 'Flore Pleno'	1 /60	Achillea ptarmica
⑱	Rubus spectabilis	1 /300	R. 'Benenden'
⑲	Salix hastata 'Wehrhahnii'	1 /200	S. purpurea
⑳	Trollius chinensis	5 /90	T. x cultorum hybrids

Qty: the number of specimens used in this recipe; numbers can be adjusted to suit a different site.
Space: recommended spacings for optimum growth (in centimetres).

▲ Tulips and ferns at the water's edge ensure a colourful spring display before the larger, marginal plants grow to flowering size.

❧ Besides their role in shading the surface, water lilies like this Nymphaea 'Marliacea Chromatella' make a very decorative contribution to a pond.

Asiatic or candelabra primulas, such as this P. pulverulenta, naturalize in moist conditions and so make perfect plants for water or bog gardens.

The globe flower (Trollius chinensis) grows wild in damp grassland. In a garden, all species of trollius make superb perennials for early-summer flowering.

PLANT DIRECTORY

❧ Caltha palustris
Kingcup, Marsh marigold. A relative of the buttercup that has rounded, heart-shaped foliage with toothed margins, and vivid yellow, five-petalled blooms on stems which may grow to up to 45cm (18in). There is a double form, 'Flore Pleno', and a North American variant, C. palustris var. palustris, which grows larger and is considerably more invasive. Happy in bogs or in shallow water.

❧ Hosta
Plantain lilies from China and Japan. Hostas are so intensively bred that literally thousands of cultivars are now available, though many of them resemble each other to such an extent that only an expert can tell them apart. The broad, plantain-like foliage is produced in mid-spring, followed by flowers which range from white, through pale lavender to purplish-blue. Larger forms such as 'Sum and Substance' and the species H. sieboldiana provide excellent architectural foliage. Happiest on moist land, but horribly susceptible to slug damage which, since the leaves do not regenerate after the longest day, can ruin the effect for the whole summer.

❧ Iris pseudacorus
European yellow flag, Water iris. Erect sword-like leaves emerge in spring and grow to 1m (3ft) in height. The yellow 'fleur de lys' blooms arrive in early summer, on stems up to 1.5m (5ft) long. As valuable for the architectural quality of its long-lasting foliage as for its brief flowering period, I. p. 'Variegata' is even more dramatic than the natural form, having cream stripes along its leaves. These fade as they mature during the summer.

❧ Ligularia dentata
Golden groundsel. This perennial has large, rounded leaves up to 30cm (12in) across, dark green with deep purple undersides, and 1–1.5m (3–5ft) stems topped with bright orange to yellow flowers in late summer. L. glabrescens 'Gregynog Gold' is a worthy companion, with all-green leaves, similarly rounded, and bright golden-yellow flowers in early autumn. Moist soil is essential, but watch out for slugs.

❧ Lysichiton americanum
A bog plant with large yellow arum-like spathes in spring, followed by huge shiny leaves which will sometimes exceed 1m (3ft) in height. There is an Asian species, L. camtschatcensis, with white spathes.

❧ Nymphaea
Water lilies. A huge group of valuable aquatics with rhizomes that grow in the mud at the bottom of the water and produce floating, rounded leaves. It is important to suit the varieties to the dimensions of your pond. The pink N. 'Lucida', for instance, is vigorous, with a single season's spread of 1.5m (5ft), and is therefore best for a large pond. 'Froebelii' is also pink but less vigorous, spreading by 1m (3ft) in a season. For handsome, mottled foliage, try the gold-bloomed 'Aurora' and for bronzed foliage the primrose-yellow-bloomed 'Marliacea Chromatella'.

HANGING GARDENS

◄ *Corydalis cheilanthifolia* is a free-seeding perennial which colonizes wall crevices or poor soil. The emerging foliage is coppery, turning green as it matures.

► Tumbling cascades of colour, in late spring, have transformed this dry stone wall into a glorious vertical garden. The richest colours come from bellflowers and cranesbills. During quieter times, their foliage makes a gentle background for the cream and yellow corydalis, which can be encouraged to flower throughout the growing season.

This is a beautiful example of a well-planned vertical garden. Many of the plants – the hieraceums, for example, and the ferny-leaved corydalis – have attractive foliage, whereas the cerise cranesbills, blue campanulas and red to purple aubrietas add to the intensity of the colours. For much of the year, the planting is so lush that the stone wall all but disappears, but its solid structure supports the planting in summer and makes a pleasing winter feature in itself when the vegetation has died down.

Vertical planting need never limit itself to climbers or wall shrubs. Wherever there is an opportunity to grow plants in vertical surfaces, without risking structural damage, the results will be pleasing and distinctive. With small plants – especially those which are fragrant – the added appeal is that when they furnish the sides of a wall, or a steep bank, they are nearer the eyes and nose, and can therefore be enjoyed at close quarters.

Many of the plants here are either repeat-flowering or will reproduce several times in a season, their progeny giving rise to subsequent displays. Most species seed themselves quite freely about the wall, making it an almost self-sustaining habitat.

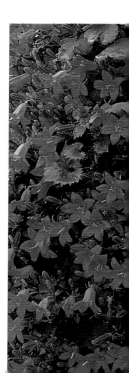

❧ Shapely in bloom, and a rich royal blue, *Campanula portenschlagiana* is one the easiest of the bellflowers, often seeding itself freely, and carries a long succession of flower, particularly during early summer. Such plants can become invasive in favourable conditions, so regular dead-heading is wise.

Planting Plan 3m x 1.5m (10ft x 5ft)

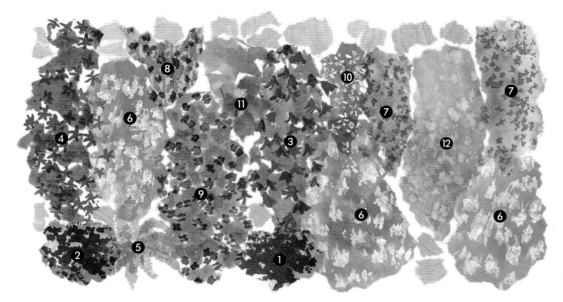

Groundwork: To get plants off to a good start, place some gritty but fertile compost into each planting hole or chink. Large, mature plants may be difficult to establish, but young seedlings or immature plants will be easier to fit into their confined growing quarters.

Planting procedure: Paint a picture with your plants! The structure is already there, so you need only add the infill, plus one or two special performers. In this planting, the colours are evenly distributed across the space, but you may prefer to group similar colours together.

Maintenance: Seeds should sow themselves into the crevices and the plants will adjust themselves to their optimum size for the spot. But watch for invasiveness: aubrieta, geranium, corydalis and *Campanula poscharskyana* are all inclined to colonize every available inch, so be ready to remove surplus specimens of these. Beware of weeds, especially perennial species, and pull these out the moment they appear. Once established, it will be hard to eliminate them without damage to the rest of the planting, as creeping rootstocks can proliferate behind the stones.

PLANT DIRECTORY

✿ Aubrieta
Commonplace though it may be, this European mat-forming or trailing plant is the mainstay of the spring alpine garden. Blue, mauve or reddish-purple flowers are so densely massed on the plants that, in spring, the foliage is all but blotted out. It is a free seeder, but named varieties must be propagated vegetatively if their colours are to remain true. Popular with early-flying butterflies and bees.

✿ Campanula portenschlagiana
This is just one of the many bellflowers ideal for alpine conditions. The foliage is rounded to heart-shaped, irregularly lobed and sometimes toothed. The rich, royal-blue to purple flowers are large in relation to the plants, and therefore make a conspicuous display. Easy to propagate, either from seed or from divisions.

✿ Corydalis cheilanthifolia
Perennial, but a vigorous seeder with deeply divided, fern-like foliage, brownish or reddish when young, and successions of deep yellow flower-spikes. May succumb to very hard weather, but seed left over from previous years will usually germinate, once winter is over.

✿ Corydalis ochroleuca
A valuable plant for growing in chinks in walls, or on stony ground. It has vivid green, lobed, much divided foliage which, though easily bruised, is quick to regenerate. The curious double-lipped, cream-coloured blooms are thickly crowded on short stems and are produced throughout the season, though with a main flush in spring. The darker yellow *C. lutea* is a closely related species.

✿ In the wild, aubrieta is almost always blue-mauve but this variety, 'April Joy', is magenta. To flower this profusely, aubrietas like limy soil and full sun in very sharp-draining soil.

✿ Pale cream blooms tipped with darker yellow, held above finely divided, ferny foliage make *Corydalis ochroleuca* a handsome wall plant. Its flowering lasts the entire growing season.

Ingredients

Key	Plant	Qty/Space (cm)	Substitute
①	Aubrieta 'April Joy'	3 /30	Arabis ferdinandi-coburgi
②	Aubrieta x cultorum	>5 /30	Aurinia saxatilis (yellow)
③	Campanula portenschlagiana	>3 /20	C. carpatica
④	Campanula poscharskyana	>2 /20	C. cochleariifolia
⑤	Corydalis cheilanthifolia	>3 /30	Polystichum setiferum Divisilobum
⑥	Corydalis ochroleuca	>5 /30	C. lutea
⑦	Daphne cneorum	1 /45	Chamaecytisus purpureus
⑧	Dianthus gratianopolitanus	>3 /20	D. deltoides
⑨	Geranium macrorrhizum 'Bevan's Variety'	3 /30	G. x cantabrigiensis
⑩	Geranium renardii	1 /30	Antirrhinum sempervirens
⑪	Hieraceum lanatum	1 /30	Verbascum 'Letitia'
⑫	Origanum vulgare 'Aureum'	1 /20	O. rotundifolium

Qty: *the number of specimens used in this recipe; numbers can be adjusted to suit a different site.*
Space: *recommended spacings for optimum growth (in centimetres).*

ORNAMENTAL GRASSES

◄ Among the largest grasses, cortaderias create a dramatic display from mid- or late summer, when their silvery inflorescences begin to emerge, right through the depths of winter. Being native to the high Andes mountains, they are perfectly frost-hardy but, since they can look untidy in the off-season, are best sited at the back of a border.

Grasses have a language all their own. Their leaves etch thin, curving lines against the background; their flower stems erupt in arcs that cascade out from the plants, making handsome outlines which dance and sway in the slightest breeze. Even their sound is distinctive – a gentle rustling in light winds, but in stronger weather they sigh and hiss like animate beings. Wonderful subjects for lawns and as background plants, grasses are effective for plant compositions to delight through the year.

► A startling combination, composed chiefly of ornamental grasses and grass-like plants, is seen here in full, glorious bloom. And it looks as delightful in winter, when the grasses have dried off and are dusted with hoar frost, as in summer. Grasses are indisputably the stars here, but their special character is brought out by careful placing of such contrast plants as sedums, asters and Japanese anemones. Colours are carefully managed too, with silvery foliage placed to contrast with bronze and pink flowers, making a clean contrast with the more diffuse colours of the grasses.

Grasses almost plant themselves. Their natural beauty is striking but, with thoughtful planning, these attributes can be even further enhanced. The use of low-growing, mat-forming plants in this composition has resulted in a low-profile, bronze and silver understorey, allowing the grasses to be the star performers. Apart from an unusual but effective background of pines, and a single metal frame, these grasses create the planting's outline and framework. Soft, changeable and impermanent they may be, but they dominate the entire planting, making every other species subordinate.

An advantage to such a planting is that the results are speedy, transforming the area in a single season, especially once the grasses are in flower. This planting relies on large grasses like miscanthus and cortaderia but you could scale down the dimensions by using smaller species, like hakonechloa, molinia or festuca.

Groundwork: Any reasonable soil will suit the majority of grasses, as long as it has been dug over, and preferably improved with compost or other organic material. But for the grasses shown, moist conditions — or at least a moderate summer rainfall — are desirable and mulching is important for moisture retention. The ground-cover plants will also help to keep in moisture.

Planting procedure: The concept of tiering — short plants in front, tall at the back — has been all but abandoned here, resulting in a superb sense of drama, with a dominant tall grass in the foreground and smaller plants peeping out from behind. The tallest and strongest-growing species — pennisetum, cortaderia, phormium and miscanthus — are the main anchor plants. To ensure these get off to a good start, include some bonemeal at planting time. Space the background plants evenly, to encourage them to merge.

Maintenance: One of the joys of this kind of planting is to watch the gradual changes taking place as the seasons pass. The temptation to tidy things up in autumn must therefore be resisted. Early spring will be a better time to work through the bed, getting rid of dead or unsightly material. Even then, it will not be necessary to remove all the previous year's growth. Evergreen species can simply be tidied by pulling away dead foliage. These grasses are all hardy except for the pennisetum, which is slightly tender and may need winter protection.

All grasses, but especially large, robust species, are hungry feeders, with an almost unlimited response to high-nitrogen fertilizer. You need to exercise caution, however, since overfeeding can have a coarsening effect, the growth becoming so rampant as to threaten the background plants. Flowers look smaller on overfed grasses, and foliage colours may be less interesting, so feed only moderately.

Future: Grasses can become untidy, and many are invasive. Those with a creeping rootstock, for example the miscanthus, will need to be kept within bounds. When a tussock-forming grass grows old and unthrifty, replace it with a younger plant.

Fleshy leaves and flattened flowerheads make a soothing contrast to all the grasses. And in winter, this *Sedum spectabile* will continue its display as it dries, making a distinctive outline in the bed.

Grass-like foliage enables this *Schizostylis coccinea* to harmonize with the other grasses and sedges, but the coral-red flowers, produced in succession in autumn, make a seasonal feature.

An oat relative, *Stipa tenuissima* has leaves and flower stems that are so narrow as to appear like golden-green filaments.

Planting Plan   6m x 4.5m (20ft x 15ft)

▶ Though unrelated to grasses, New Zealand flax (*Phormium tenax*) has a number of grass-like qualities. The leaves are sword-shaped, long and flat with a central crease, and come in rich, warm colours. In the wind they rustle and wave like grasses, and in winter they create a shapely outline. Phormiums are not hardy in extreme cold.

Plants with pink, blue or purple flowers harmonize well with grasses, especially in late summer when the greens are turning to gold. This is *Aster amellus*, a tough, long-lasting perennial.

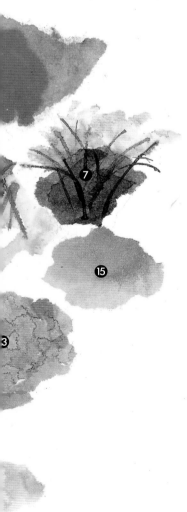

Ingredients

▼

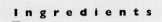

Key	Plant	Qty/Space (cm)	Substitute
①	Anemone × hybrida 'Honorine Jobert'	5 /60	Chrysanthemum uliginosum
②	Artemisia stelleriana	>3 /45	Senecio viravira
③	Aster amellus	5 /45	A. × frikartii 'Mönch'
④	Cortaderia selloana 'Sunningdale Silver'	1 /150	C. s. 'Pumila'
⑤	Helichrysum angustifolium	>3 /75	Lavandula lanata
⑥	Miscanthus floridulus	<3 /100	M. sacchariflorus
⑦	Miscanthus sinensis 'Silberfeder'	<3 /100	M. s. 'Zebrinus'
⑧	Pennisetum alopecuroides	1 /75	P. villosum
⑨	Phormium tenax	1 /120	P. 'Bronze Baby'
⑩	Pinus radiata	hedge /300	P. coulteri
⑪	Rosa glauca	1 /150	Buddleja 'Lochinch'
⑫	Schizostylis coccinea	>3 /45	S. c. 'Jennifer'
⑬	Sedum spectabile	>3 /45	S. telephium
⑭	Sedum 'Ruby Glow'	<5 /20	S. 'Vera Jameson'
⑮	Stipa tenuissima	<5 /20	S. calamagrostis

Qty: *the number of specimens used in this recipe; numbers can be adjusted to suit a different site.*
Space: *recommended spacings for optimum growth (in centimetres).*

PLANT DIRECTORY

❧ *Anemone × hybrida*
Tall, durable perennials bearing a profusion of pink or white blooms in late summer and into autumn. *A. × h.* 'Honorine Jobert' is one of the finest, with lobed leaves and stems which may grow to almost 2m (6ft), many of them branched and generously furnished with white flowers, each with a centre of golden stamens. Happy even in poor soil, they are inclined to spread if not restrained.

❧ *Cortaderia selloana*
Pampas grass. A coarse, vigorous grass from South America whose leaves, if stroked the wrong way, can cut like a razor. The flowers, which begin to emerge in the second half of summer and persist through winter, are creamy with a silvery sheen. 'Sunningdale Silver' is one of the finest varieties, but 'Rendatleri' has pinkish flowers.

❧ *Miscanthus sinensis*
A big, dramatic grass with tall, gaunt stems which, in the right conditions, will reach almost 4m (13ft). The leaves are borne along the stems, many of them having a paler central stripe. In the variety 'Zebrinus', the leaves and stems are punctuated with yellowish bands.

❧ *Pennisetum alopecuroides*
Basal clumps of soft, narrow leaves create a large tussock out of which the foxtail blooms erupt in summer. When young, these are purplish but, as they mature, silvery whiskers develop, softening their outlines and creating an airy effect.

❧ *Phormium tenax*
New Zealand flax. Not related to the grasses, in spite of having long, flexible, strap-like leaves. These can be purplish or, in the case of such variegated varieties as 'Dazzler' or 'Sundowner', striped in varying hues of pink, cream or yellow. On mature plants, the flower spikes may reach a dramatic height – even 10m (40ft) or more – but these plants will not tolerate sustained frost.

❧ *Schizostylis coccinea*
From Southern Africa, this relative of the iris has sword-shaped leaves and elegant flower stems that reach 25cm (10in) in length, carrying successions of coral-red blooms which last from early autumn to early winter. Prefers moist soil but a warm position. Good varieties include 'Major', possibly the largest of the group, and 'Jennifer', the flowers of which are shell-pink.

❧ *Sedum spectabile*
One of the most valuable herbaceous plants in cultivation, because of its fresh green, succulent foliage which develops from early spring and its flat-topped umbels of bright pink flowers which come out in late summer and persist throughout autumn. Even when decorated with winter frost, these look beautiful. Happy in most soils, in full sun, they must be divided regularly – at least every 3 years – to ensure stocky plants which will not flop over.

SPRING PALETTE

◄ The long succession of spring bulbs – from crocus and scillas, which show before the equinox – moves to its climax at the height of the season when the tulips are at their best. Double varieties are usually shorter and more stocky than other tulips, but their flowers are almost always longer-lasting. This form is 'Lilac Perfection'.

Lightness of touch, combined with strict colour control and a harmonious arrangement of plants give this springtime border a joyous air. There are plenty of blues and creams to keep the colour scheme cool, but with golden foliage and dottings of purple and mauve the effect is fresh and welcoming.

An abundance of small flowers, particularly from forget-me-nots, honesty and wallflowers, ensures a naturalistic display but the strong framework created by trellis structures and clipped shrubs gives shape and body to the design. Large drumstick garlics provide an extra flourish of drama, and plenty more lies in store for the rest of summer.

▲ Dark purple flowers make a dramatic contrast with paler blooms and there are few as dark as the so-called 'black' tulips. 'Queen of Night' – a Darwin hybrid – stands out well among the blue forget-me-nots and ivory wallflowers.

◄ The arrangement of plants is subtly tiered, with changing textures in different layers. Frothy explosions of forget-me-nots fill the spaces between flowering tulips and the leaves of such later-blooming perennials as irises and cranesbills. Further back, the vivid *Spiraea japonica* 'Goldflame' becomes a spring star performer, its young shoots tinged with orange, while behind, the gaunt stems of the Mediterranean spurge (*Euphorbia characias*) are partially hidden among foliage.

Since the majority of perennials flower in summer, developing a mature display early in the year presents an interesting challenge. Here, in spite of limited dimensions, a varied collection of flowers blooms against a strong background of formal shapes and structures, backed by an attractive stone wall. Golden-leaved hops are beginning to climb an old timber framework and, further along, a wooden trellis obelisk awaits its furnishing of summer climbers. The structure of this planting is completed with a formally clipped holly (*Ilex* × *altaclerensis* 'Lawsoniana'), a female tree whose berries will complement its golden-variegated foliage in winter.

As with all good understorey plantings, foliage plays as important a role as flower. There is a fascinating interplay of textures here, with plenty of sword-like foliage from the bulbs and from Siberian irises which will bloom later. They make a stark contrast with the fussiness of the flower sprays and give a dark foil to the golden hues of spurge – two species are here – and a golden robinia.

Planting Plan   2.5m x 7m (8ft x 23ft)

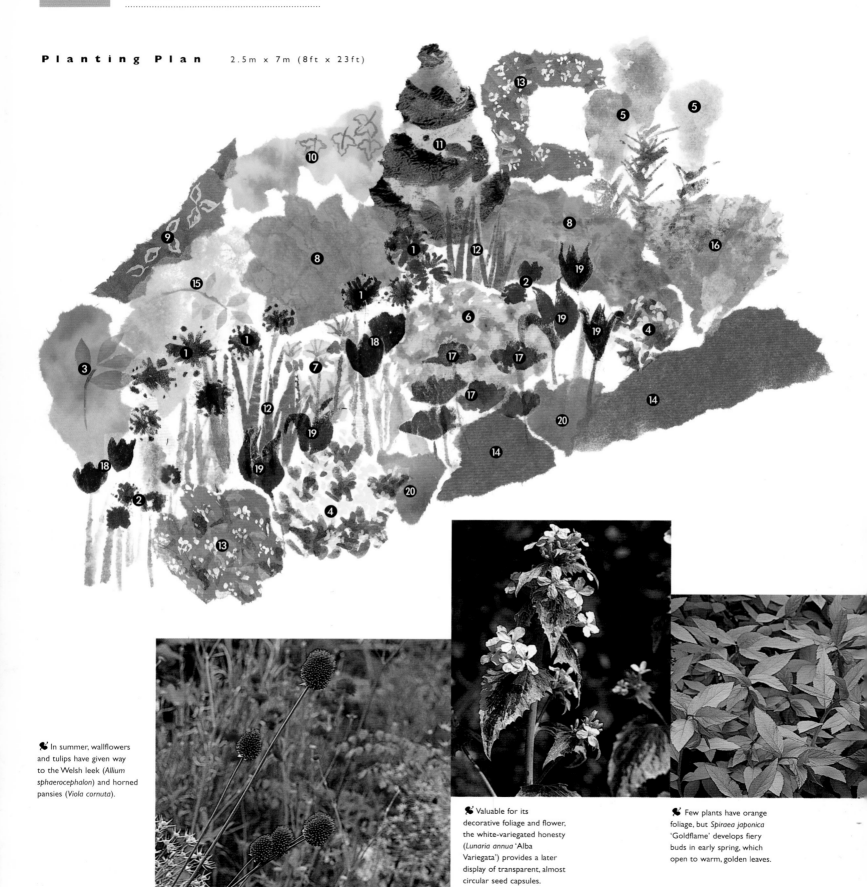

❧ In summer, wallflowers and tulips have given way to the Welsh leek (*Allium sphaerocephalon*) and horned pansies (*Viola cornuta*).

❧ Valuable for its decorative foliage and flower, the white-variegated honesty (*Lunaria annua* 'Alba Variegata') provides a later display of transparent, almost circular seed capsules.

❧ Few plants have orange foliage, but *Spiraea japonica* 'Goldflame' develops fiery buds in early spring, which open to warm, golden leaves.

Ingredients

Key	Plant	Qty/Space (cm)	Substitute
1	Allium rosenbachianum	>20 /30	A. giganteum
2	Allium hollandicum 'Purple Sensation'	>20 /30	A. cristophii
3	Cornus alba 'Aurea'	1 /200	C. a. 'Sibirica'
4	Erysimum cheiri 'Ivory White'	7 /30	E. 'Moonlight'
5	Euphorbia characias	1 /60	E. palustris
6	Euphorbia polychroma	1 /45	E. wallichii
7	Fritillaria imperialis 'Maxima Lutea'	3 /45	F. persica 'Adiyaman'
8	Geranium psilostemon	1 /45	G. pratense
9	Hedera colchica 'Variegata'	1 /200	H. c. 'Sulphur Heart'
10	Humulus lupulus 'Aureus'	1 /200	Lonicera japonica 'Aureoreticulata'
11	Ilex x altaclerensis 'Lawsoniana'	1 /300	I. x a. 'Belgica Aurea'
12	Iris sibirica	3 /60	I. spuria
13	Lunaria annua 'Alba Variegata'	>3 /45	L. rediviva
14	Myosotis alpestris	>20 /20	Omphalodes verna
15	Robinia pseudoacacia 'Frisia'	1 /300	Gleditsia triacanthos 'Sunburst'
16	Spiraea japonica 'Goldflame'	1 /200	Philadelphus coronarius 'Aureus'
17	Tulipa 'Lilac Perfection'	10 /20	Any paeony-flowered tulip
18	Tulipa 'Queen of Night'	10 /20	T. 'Negrita'
19	Tulipa 'Maytime'	10 /20	T. 'Ballade'
20	Viola 'Maggie Mott'	>3 /30	V. 'Huntercombe Purple'

Qty: *the number of specimens used in this recipe; numbers can be adjusted to suit a different site.*
Space: *recommended spacings for optimum growth (in centimetres).*

Consider broadening the season a little by introducing some later-flowering climbers. The alliums should multiply by seeding, but tulip numbers tend to decline over the years, so be ready to add a few extra each autumn.

Wallflowers, once the mainstay of formal spring bedding, can be used to add substance to a mixed border. This variety is *Erysimum cheiri* 'Ivory White'.

Yellow-leaved plants like the golden hop (*Humulus lupulus* 'Aureus') are never as gold as when the first young leaves emerge. The colour works best in gentle shade.

Groundwork: When developing a border like this from scratch, first ensure that the ground is clear of weeds. If the smallest trace of any perennial weed species remains, delay your planting, because once it is established it will be extremely difficult to prevent a troublesome build-up. The soil should be in good heart too, its level of organic matter enhanced by the addition of well-rotted manure or compost.

Planting procedure: This is a border to build up rather than create in a single season. Nevertheless, a magnificent display is still perfectly feasible even in the first season. First place the framework plants, like the holly, robinia and *Cornus alba*. You might want to adjust the position of these, and of the man-made structures, as their final placing will influence the appearance of the whole display. But bear in mind the overall effect, rather than treating each element in isolation.

Plant allium bulbs any time in autumn but tulips in late autumn or early winter, to avoid the risk of tulip fire. Plant as randomly as you like, in small groups of unequal numbers, with one or two individuals standing apart. Create drifts of one species, rather than mixing the bulbs up.

Maintenance: Diligent work in autumn will reward you with a fine spring flourish, but with so many permanent bulbs in the ground, and with plants encouraged to self-sow, it will not be possible to dig this plot through without inflicting damage. Restrict your maintenance activities, therefore, to surface treatment. Any mulch should be light, as your aim is to encourage seedlings. Remove all dead and dying material before the onset of winter.

PLANT DIRECTORY

Allium
Large tribe of ornamental onions, mostly flowering in late spring and early summer. Colours are usually in the pink and purple range, though blue, yellow and white alliums are also common. *A. aflatunense* and *A. hollandicum* 'Purple Sensation' both grow to 1m (3ft) tall, with vivid purple drumstick flowers, but there are lower-growing species too. The leaves of most alliums die back at flowering, so plant them among subjects with luxuriant foliage.

Erysimum cheiri
Wallflower. Though grown as biennials, a number of wallflowers are perennial, albeit somewhat short-lived, and all can be raised from cuttings as well as from seed sown in early summer. Heights vary, depending on variety, but all are fragrant. Colours are yellow, scarlet, red, mauve, purple and orange. Not hardy in regions where winters are severe.

Euphorbia characias
Shrubby-looking perennials from the Mediterranean region with stiff, curved stems clothed with narrow, glaucous leaves. The golden flowerheads develop in late winter and persist well into summer, fading only when their seed has been shed. When cut or damaged, stems and leaves exude a sticky latex which is both poisonous and irritating to the skin. Easy to propagate from seed or cuttings and happy growing anywhere, even on the poorest of soils.

Humulus lupulus 'Aureus'
Golden hop. A vigorous, often invasive climber with a running root system and twining growth to 3m (10ft) or more. The stems are so rough to the touch that they can scratch; flowers in female plants resemble pale green pine cones and are deliciously aromatic – but more so after they have been dried for use in brewing than when live on the plant.

Lunaria annua
Honesty. So-called because its seed capsules resemble translucent purses through which the seeds, like tiny coins, are visible. In good soil, plants will grow to 1m (3ft) high, with broad, toothed leaves and branched stems of purple or white flowers, each with four petals. In *L. a.* 'Alba Variegata' the leaves are stippled and splashed with creamy-white markings. Will self-sow freely, after an initial planting.

Robinia pseudoacacia
False acacia. Medium-sized to large tree with late-emerging pinnate leaves and, in mature specimens, white, sweet-scented pea-flower blossoms. The form 'Frisia' has golden foliage and long, somewhat brittle stems which move gracefully in the breeze. Totally frost-hardy, but happiest in a sheltered position.

Spiraea japonica
A dome-shaped, deciduous shrub, growing to 1.5m (5ft) with umbels of pink or white flowers. A good pink form is 'Anthony Waterer' but better for foliage colour and for a neater, more compact habit is 'Goldflame', whose young, emerging leaves are orange to bronze, turning paler gold as they mature.

A WOODLAND SCENE

▶ Unlike the more conspicuous white-flowered wake-robin, this form of *Trillium sessile* has dark russet-brown flowers. The narrow petals are held erect above triple leaves that are interestingly veined and marked. Moist, leafy soil is essential for this plant which, even in ideal conditions, can be slow to establish.

A walk in the woods on a sunny spring day allows you to experience all the glory of the shade-loving flora. Similar woodland conditions prevail around the world, so although native plant species vary from one continent to another, their appearance has much in common. In Europe, for example, wood anemones, oxlips or bluebells might make up the bulk of a woodland flower population, whereas in North America a similar display may come from foam flowers, wake-robins and columbines. This shade planting represents a tiny fragment of North American forest.

▲ Solomon's seal (*Polygonatum x hybridum*), so-called because the marks on its rhizomes resemble royal seals, is one of the woodland plants found in both the New and the Old Worlds. Though the pendant, green-tipped white flowers are short-lived in spring, the arching stems and handsome foliage last well into the autumn, often producing crops of small red fruits along their length.

◄ This section of North American woodland is a shining example of native plants put to excellent garden use. Though most species are from North America, they are all available from commercial nurseries in other countries, so an identical arrangement could be planted anywhere. Forget-me-nots and foam flowers (*Tiarella*) provide the bulk of the colour in mid-spring, with the soft lavender and blue tints replicated in the Virginian bluebells and a beautiful creeping phlox (*P. stolonifera*). In contrast, the American columbine adds a dash of fiery warmth with its red and yellow blooms.

The art of woodland planting is to achieve a natural look. And a useful way of finding out exactly what that is would be to study a genuine woodland and see just how the plants arrange themselves. If you are lucky enough to have in your garden natural shade from trees, light levels will vary across the ground from dense shade to almost full light. In the wild, different species dominate in various spots, according to the conditions that suit them, and it is important to mimic this natural variation in a garden setting.

This garden achieves an authentic re-creation of a woodland. The plants are all New World natives and the way they grow in the wild has been closely observed and imitated. But the effect is enhanced by planting key species in bolder groups than might occur in the wild. The columbines have been gathered together to make a strong focal point, first with their ferny foliage, then with the reddish blooms which link spring to summer. The mertensias make conspicuous statements too, their large leaves and vivid blue flowers contrasting with the white drifts of tiarella. But other species – like forget-me-nots and violets – are encouraged to seed randomly, making a naturalistic background.

All woodland gardens are at their best in spring, since plants growing under deciduous trees must flower and set seed before the leaf canopy develops overhead and blocks out the light. So to extend interest into summer and autumn, you will need plenty of foliage plants. Ferns are useful here and there are species that enjoy both dry and moist shade.

Planting Plan   6m x 3.5m (20ft x 12ft)

Ingredients

Key	Plant	Qty/Space (cm)	Substitute
①	*Arisaema triphyllum*	>3 /45	*A. jacquemontii*
②	*Aquilegia canadensis*	>5 /30	*A. flavescens*
③	*Dryopteris affinis*	>3 /60	*D. wallichiana*
④	*Matteuccia struthiopteris*	>3 /60	*Polystichum setiferum*
⑤	*Mertensia pulmonarioides*	>3 /30	*Symphytum x uplandicum*
⑥	*Myosotis sylvestris*	>10 /20	*Pulmonaria officinalis*
⑦	*Phlox stolonifera*	>3 /20	*P. s. 'Ariane'*
⑧	*Polygonatum x hybridum*	>5 /45	*Smilacina racemosa*
⑨	*Tiarella cordifolia*	>30 /30	*T. trifoliata*
⑩	*Trillium sessile*	>3 /30	*T. erectum*
⑪	*Viola sororia*	>5 /20	*V. odorata*

Qty: *the number of specimens used in this recipe; numbers can be adjusted to suit a different site.*
Space: *recommended spacings for optimum growth (in centimetres).*

❦ Because they bloom in shade, many woodland plants come in pale colours. *Tiarella cordifolia* produces drifts of foamy white blooms in spring,

Forget-me-nots (*Myosotis sylvestris*) are so common in spring bedding schemes that it is easy to forget that they originate in the woods and will naturalize happily in dappled shade.

► As fern leaves unfurl in spring, their colours and shapes run through a series of subtle changes. In the fiddle-head stage shown here, the fronds of *Matteuccia struthiopteris* are tightly curled in on themselves and coated with a dusting of fine, rusty scales. But as the stem extends, the bright green leaflets expand, each one further divided to create a graceful tracery.

❧ North America is home to several distinctive columbine species. *Aquilegia canadensis* makes a beautiful woodland subject, both for its spurred flowers in spring and for its ferny foliage.

❧ A close relative of the forget-me-not, *Mertensia pulmonarioides* resents disturbance. Once it is established, however, and in the right conditions, the plants will self-sow readily.

Groundwork: With a huge quantity of leaves falling each year and rotting down to make leafmould, it is unsurprising that most woodland soil is rich in organic material. So when developing a woodland garden, it is important to build up the soil's organic content. It is easy to make leafmould by simply composting all fallen foliage, but this takes time. Bought-in mulches of bark chippings or shredded plant material will also help you to develop the soil.

Be sparing with fertilizer or manure. All these woodland plants are wildlings and need no extra feed. If the soil is too rich, many will grow out of character, with too much leaf and stem and too little flower.

Planting procedure: Planting in drifts looks more natural than cramped clumps, but you should plant as though the drifts had seeded naturally, rather than mix everything up. Do not let the quest for random planting wipe out your artistic sensibilities, however. Bold drifts, especially of tiarella and phlox, and ferns in generous clumps make a stronger statement than might occur in the wild. But let the distribution of prominent plants like the arisaemas be totally random — never measure out spacings or distribute too evenly.

Maintenance: To encourage self-seeding, allow dying flower stems to dry completely and shake them about over the soil before removing them. Be vigilant against weeds and eliminate before they have a chance to seed.

PLANT DIRECTORY

❧ *Aquilegia* (New World species)
Columbines from the New World tend to occur in warm colours — red, yellow, cream or pink — and in bicolours. *A. canadensis*, a common North American woodlander, grows 30–40cm (12–16in) high and bears red and yellow flowers, each with a set of five hooked spurs, making them resemble perching birds. Other New World species include the long-spurred, yellow-flowered *A. flavescens*. All are hardy perennials, easily raised from seed.

❧ *Dryopteris affinis*
Golden male fern. This fern with a 'shuttlecock' formation is very nearly evergreen, with bipinnate fronds that grow fairly erect and, in reasonable soil, reach a height of almost 1m (3ft). As they mature, the fronds turn a darker green and acquire soft, rust-coloured scales along the backs of their midribs. As well as the wild species, there are several garden forms.

❧ *Mertensia pulmonarioides*
Virginia bluebell. A moisture-loving woodlander common in the American Midwest, with glabrous foliage and 60–90cm (2–3ft) stems bearing nodding blue flowers which are pink in the bud. Can be difficult to establish in some soils, but worth growing because it is much more refined than the European blue comfrey (*Symphytum × uplandicum*) which it so closely resembles.

❧ *Tiarella cordifolia*
Foam flower. A creeping, sometimes invasive root-stock enables this native of North America to form wide mats of soft green, lobed foliage topped, in spring, by drifts of white, foamy blooms on 25cm (10in) stems. In autumn the foliage takes on a russet or reddish hue. This is a plant that needs freedom to spread, if it is to look its best.

❧ *Trillium sessile*
Toad shade, Wake-robin. A perennial that forms clumps — though it takes time — with 30cm (12in) stems bearing leaves which always grow in threes. These form a ruff below the flowers whose petals also come in two sets of three. The leaves of this shade-lover are blotched in brown, and the flowers are a sombre, brownish maroon. Moist soil enriched with leafmould is essential. The white-flowered *T. grandiflorum* is a brighter alternative.

❧ *Viola sororia*
Although common in woodland, this North American violet is also happy in a sunny spot. Short, stubby rhizomes produce 10cm (4in) stems topped with heart-shaped leaves or with large flowers in strong colours of sky-blue, violet-blue or white. Forms with freckled flowers occur too. This viola is a free-seeder, with the violet characteristic of producing self-fertilized seed capsules in late summer from flower buds that have never opened.

A DRY GRAVEL GARDEN

Stony or gravelly stretches are common in natural landscapes, along river beds, in mountain screes or as part of the desert. In a garden setting, gravel makes a sympathetic growing medium for a surprisingly wide range of plants. In very hot, dry conditions, succulents and other drought-tolerant species would not look amiss but even where rainfall is higher, gravel still makes a beautiful and natural-looking background for small shrubs, summer-flowering perennials, annuals and winter- and spring-flowering bulbs.

◀ A superb selection of *Rudbeckia hirta* with glowing mahogany rays lightening to rich marmalade at their tips. These short-lived perennials are best propagated from seed, removing progeny which does not come true to the parents.

▲ An intriguing succulent from north-west Africa, *Aeonium arboreum* can grow into a shrub more than 1m (3ft) high. In the wild they are green, but this dark garden selection with fleshy, purple-bronze leaves is 'Atropurpureum'.

▶ A walled yard has been transformed into a delightful gravel garden, planted to provide colour and interest throughout the year. Although it has a permanent look, many of the plants are frost-tender and are lifted for overwintering each autumn. Colour is dotted about, rather than composed in complementary groups, but there is a loose theme which embraces the duskier tones of reddish orange and yellow, as picked up in the rudbeckias, the golden grass in the foreground and the magnificent deep purple succulent, *Aeonium arboreum* 'Atropurpureum'. Small, trailing or self-seeding plants such as New Zealand burr and fleabane have been encouraged to colonize the spaces between the statelier specimens.

An interesting mix of textures, colours and shapes gives this gravel garden its distinctive feel. Apart from the rose – a startling addition – the plants are all drought-resistant and will thrive on neglect. The planting's structure comes from the brick wall and the large climbing roses along the outside, and additionally from such architectural plants as the aeonium, the young fan palm just behind it and even some of the taller perennials. The stone sink makes a pleasing focal point and the absence of a dividing line between pathway and growing area encourages one to move in among the plants – a delightful added bonus being that you are able to touch, feel and smell the plants at close quarters.

The understorey consists mainly of plant subjects that have been allowed either to spread themselves around or to self-sow. Given time, large areas of the gravel may well become completely covered with vegetation, but this should not be a problem as long as the overall sense of openness and accessibility remains.

Planting Plan
10m x 15m (33ft x 50ft)

Ingredients

Key	Plant	Qty/Space (cm)	Substitute
1	Acaena microphylla 'Copper Carpet'	>3 /30	A. adscendens 'Glaucens'
2	Aeonium arboreum 'Atropurpureum'	1 /100	A. arboreum
3	Agapanthus campanulatus	1 /60	A. inapertus
4	Arctotis x hybrida	>3 /45	Ursinia anthemoides
5	Cotyledon orbiculata	>3 /45	Crassula arborescens
6	Erigeron karvinskianus	>5 /20	Anthemis punctata cupaniana
7	Euphorbia characias	>3 /120	E. x martinii
8	Foeniculum vulgare	>5 /100	F. vulgare 'Purpureum'
9	Gazania hybrid	>3 /30	G. krebsiana
10	Hebe brachysiphon	1 /90	Genista hispanica
11	Helichrysum angustifolium	>3 /60	H. splendidum
12	Luzula sylvatica 'Aurea'	3 /45	Carex buchananii
13	Malvastrum lateritium	1 /60	Sphaeralcea munroana
14	Melianthus major	1 /90	Helleborus argutifolius
15	Phormium tenax 'Bronze Baby'	1 /100	Carex comans
16	Rosa 'Flower Carpet'	1 /100	Cistus corbariensis
17	Rudbeckia hirta (selected form)	> 5 /45	Gaillardia
18	Solanum aviculare	1 /120	S. rantonnetii
19	Trachycarpus fortunei	1	Chamaerops humilis
20	Tropaeolum majus	5 /60	T. polyphyllum

Qty: the number of specimens used in this recipe; numbers can be adjusted to suit a different site.
Space: recommended spacings for optimum growth (in centimetres).

❧ Striking because of its unusual colouring, this specially selected rudbeckia is short-lived as a perennial but will come fairly true from seed collected in late summer.

❧ An easy plant, either for a dry scree garden or to encourage to seed around in an old wall, Erigeron karvinskianus produces a succession of small, daisy-like flowers all summer.

◀ **A mix of succulents, roses and aromatic greenery give a luxuriant look to this hot, dry site. Providing a display of fleshy grey foliage and umbels of pendant, bell-like flowers is** *Cotyledon orbiculata*, **a plant that needs to be frost-free in winter.**

Groundwork: Gravel is useful for creating a uniform surface and disguising what might lie beneath. You must always adapt your choice of plants to the type of soil you have. Drought-tolerant species like these will be quite happy in impoverished soil but will not tolerate poor drainage. And gravel will not in itself solve drainage problems. To do that, you need to ensure that water can run away, by incorporating porous material such as grit or compost into the soil itself or, in extreme cases, by installing an underground drainage system. But gravel will help to keep rot-prone plant species like those from arid Mediterranean regions dry round the neck.

Planting procedure: Planting in gravel hardly differs from digging into a more conventional border, except that you have to scrape the stones away first, to stop them falling into the planting hole. After planting, do not be alarmed if soil contaminates the stony surface: rain will soon wash it back into the ground.

Maintenance: Tender plants, particularly the succulents, will need winter protection, but since many are slow-growing you can save yourself time and trouble by plunging the containers directly into the ground. Make sure water can drain right through the pots.

Running a sharp hoe through the shingle will control both weeds and the excess of volunteer seedlings that will appear after a couple of seasons. But hoeing can be indiscriminate, and it may be better to weed by hand, simply removing any unwelcome seedlings. These plants are not hungry feeders but if you feel they are languishing, sprinkle a little blood, fish and bonemeal or granular fertilizer — manure will not work — over the shingle in spring.

PLANT DIRECTORY

❧ *Aeonium arboreum*
A gorgeous, frost-tender succulent native to North Africa which, given time, will develop into a uniquely shaped bush, up to 2m (6ft) high. The stems can be brittle but, if broken off accidentally, simply push the stem end into the ground and stand back while it takes root. Panicles of yellow flowers appear on mature plants in spring.

❧ *Arctotis*
South African members of the daisy family with greyish, somewhat downy foliage and startling flowers which can be orange, pink, red or bicolour. *A. × hybrida* has some of the brightest cultivars and seed series, including 'China Rose' (soft pink) and 'Flame' (vivid scarlet-orange). It grows to around 60cm (2ft) and is frost-tender.

❧ *Erigeron karvinskianus*
A lovable weed with a creeping rootstock which has slightly hairy, grey-green leaves from which spring masses of wiry little stems carrying yellow-eyed daisy flowers. As they open, and again as they fade, these are flushed pink, but when at their peak they are white, creating gently dappled drifts, much like scattered apple blossom in summer. The plant seeds freely and is excellent for growing in old walls.

❧ *Gazania*
Low-growing, South African members of the daisy tribe which, when open to the sun, can reveal vivid orange, golden-yellow or pink blooms, often with distinctive green markings at their petal bases. The species, *G. krebsiana*, is flame-red in the wild, but there are many interesting seed series and cuttings-raised varieties.

❧ *Malvastrum lateritium*
A spreading perennial which roots as it goes, soon forming a dense carpet of low-growing stems which carry relatively large, three-lobed green leaves and solitary, peach-coloured mallow flowers. The leaves can grow too big for the flowers, so the plant fares better if half-starved, to keep the leaves small.

❧ *Rudbeckia hirta*
Coneflower. A short-lived perennial, usually grown as an annual, whose big, daisy-shaped flowers have rays in warm marmalade hues — orange, russet, yellow or brown — with such dark centres that they look black. In single varieties, the outer rays reflex elegantly, but the coneflower shown is a semi-double form, selected for its unique cinnamon colouring. Best reproduced from seed since these perennials last such a short time.

❧ *Trachycarpus fortunei*
Chusan palm. Almost hardy, this is one of the only palms that can be grown in colder gardens. Durable, fan-shaped evergreen leaves top the plant in the classical palm pattern. Though capable of sustaining a light frost, young plants need winter protection. Since it grows slowly, the Chusan palm makes a fine container plant but mature specimens can ultimately grow to more than 20m (66ft).

Most succulents are more remarkable for their foliage than for their bloom, but this cotyledon has elegant, nodding bell-flowers held above greyish leaves.

Fiery colours on this *Echeveria elegans* make a striking contrast with the neat rosettes of fleshy blue-grey leaves. In cold climates, these need frost protection.

❧ Gazanias are perfect for a hot, dry position. In dull weather they close their flowers, so it is worth selecting at least some varieties with silvery foliage. This form is 'Circus'.

A FLOWER MEADOW

▶ Though more often associated with tilled farmland, wild poppies frequently occur in meadows, especially where the sward has been broken up by cattle or sheep. In a garden setting, this is simple to mimic by scratching the turf in places and scattering poppy seed over the resulting soil.

▶ This view of the meadow in high summer shows a soft, alluring blend of ripening grasses, aromatic herbs and wildflowers, creating the most romantic of effects. This kind of planting is doubly appealing in the days of modern farming techniques, since flower meadows have become so rare in the countryside. At different seasons, a well-managed grass garden or meadow will provide constant interest, with subtle colour changes and a succession of surprises, from naturalized bulbs in spring to late-flowering summer blooms. And since so many of the plants used here are native to the area, the meadow makes an excellent refuge for local wildlife.

The scent of new-mown hay was never as sweet as when the farmer's grasses were strewn with wildflowers. Commercial hay crops are now kept weed-free with herbicides, but people are catching on to the delights of reconstructing natural flower meadows in their gardens. Grasses may still be the most abundant plants in this kind of planting, but they make a green background for hundreds of bright dots of flower in a range of colours, from dark reds through purples and blues to vivid yellow. It is vital to plant according to the nature of the soil and while this romantic meadow features mainly moisture-loving plants, it clearly has both damp and dry zones.

Green issues and a growing concern about the effect of our lifestyle on the environment are, at last, changing our approach to the way we garden. In former ages, when formality was the fashion, the garden kept nature out; nowadays we want to welcome nature and create a sanctuary for wildlife. Although this scene looks random and relaxed, its development takes skill and planning and it will need to be managed with care and sympathy.

The meadow itself is all understorey, but the outline of this design consists of the informal framework of taller plants and shrubs around its margin. Thus, a lawn, a patch of grass or even an area of bare ground

▲ Few wild species can match the pure azure blue of cornflower (*Centaurea cyanus*). In a meadow where grass plants are sparsely populated, this annual will seed itself freely, often producing autumn-germinated plants which bloom from late spring and all through summer.

would make an ideal site at almost any scale, from a few square metres to a hectare or more. The planting creates a soft, mutable texture, suffused with flushes of colours that wax and wane as the seasons pass. Some of the flowering plants used here would be far too invasive to risk including in a mixed border, but in a meadow they are kept in check by competition from the grasses. Others are less robust and need a little encouragement. Unlike a true grass meadow, the colour in this sward has been enhanced by the inclusion of such arable 'weeds' as corn marigold and cornflower. In nature they would be driven out by the grass but here they will need to be reseeded on a regular basis.

▶ Bullrush (*Typha latifolia*) is as happy in a damp meadow as it is growing in still or slow-moving water. Though too invasive for a small garden pond, the stately, light green foliage and dark brown, velvety maces make this a perfect choice for an extensive bog or meadow garden.

Groundwork: Preparation will depend on whether you are starting from scratch or converting existing grassland. In either case, eliminate all perennial weeds and undesirable plants before introducing new species. When it comes to planting, forget about spacing or measuring out. This is to be a wild habitat, in which the plant distribution is totally random.

Existing grassland: The best approach is gently to introduce young plants directly into the turf. Each plant will need a small area (no more than 25–30cm/10–12in diameter) to be cleared of grass, to provide short-term relief from competition while they get established. Once naturalized, most plants should thrive and seed themselves. To introduce bulbs, scatter them at random on the grass, then plant where they lie, using a bulb planter or narrow trowel.

Starting from scratch: If the bare soil is fluffy, press it down or roll it until firm but not compacted. Sow grass seed very thinly, at about 30 per cent of the recommended rate, mixing wildflower seeds with it. For speedier results, plant perennials wherever you want them, after sowing. Do not be distressed if a large population of annual weeds appears: they are easy to mow off during the first season. Though young perennials will get cut back too, they will regenerate; this may even help some to develop a stronger root system.

Maintenance: This can be tricky. It will be essential to cut the sward back at least once during the season, but the stage at which you mow will depend on the flowers you wish to favour. Purely spring meadows, with cowslips, lady's smocks and spring bulbs, can be mown in midsummer once the flowers have set seed. But for later summer colour, you can leave cutting until the end of the summer or else mow early, sacrificing some of the spring material but allowing the sward to regenerate for a late-summer flourish. If you do not mow at all, the nature of the meadow will gradually change, with rank weeds taking over and, eventually, trees and shrubs appearing.

The most crucial point is never to dress meadow gardens with fertilizer. The poorer the soil, the better the wildflowers will be. Fertilizer merely feeds the grasses, which will then compete too hard with the flowers. Many wildflowers, when given fertilizer, grow out of character, becoming coarsened with too much body and too little bloom.

Planting Plan   min: 5m x 3m (16ft x 10ft)

Despite the wide choice of 'improved' garden varieties of cornflower, in colours from white through pinks and blues to deep purple-black, none has the simple charm of the vivid blue wild species.

🌿 A scourge in cornfields, where weed infestations reduce cereal crop yields, the corn marigold (*Chrysanthemum segetum*) is an enchanting subject for a flowery meadow, though too invasive for a border.

Ingredients

Key	Plant	Qty	Substitute
①	Centaurea cyanus	seed	Cynoglossum amabile
②	Centaurea scabiosa	>5	Knautia macedonica
③	Chrysanthemum segetum	seed	C. coronarium
④	Dactylis glomerata	seed	Helictotrichon pratense
⑤	Epilobium hirsutum	3	Eupatorium cannabinum
⑥	Festuca pratensis	seed	Alopecurus pratensis
⑦	Knautia arvensis	>20	Centaurea nigra
⑧	Lythrum salicaria	>5	Lysimachia vulgaris
⑨	Origanum vulgare	>20	Mentha spicata
⑩	Papaver rhoeas	seed	P. punctatum
⑪	Poa trivialis	seed	P. annua
⑫	Senecio jacobaea	3	Anthemis tinctoria
⑬	Typha latifolia	>3	Acorus calamus

Other plants to consider

	Plant	Qty	Substitute
	Agrostemma githago	seed	Malva moschata
	Cardamine pratensis	>10	Hesperis matronalis
	Fritillaria meleagris	>50	Scilla hispanica
	Lilium martagon	>5	L. chalcedonicum
	Linaria vulgaris	>5	L. dalmatica
	Primula veris	>20	P. vulgaris

Qty: *the number of specimens used in this recipe; numbers can be adjusted to suit a different site.*
Spacing: *should be totally random.*

The rosy-purple seen here in rosebay willowherb (*Epilobium angustifolium*) is a typical flower colour of midsummer. Far too invasive for safe use in a small garden, this delightful meadow plant is best cut back before the wind-borne seeds are produced.

PLANT DIRECTORY

Centaurea scabiosa
Great knapweed. This handsome meadow flower has tough, 60cm (2ft) tall stems furnished in mid- to late summer with hard, round-headed flower buds that open with curled magenta petals. In autumn and winter the seed capsules open, leaving silvery-buff, shiny receptacles in the shape of open cups. Knapweed is an invasive plant, but fine in meadows. Forms occur with white or, more rarely, pale pink blooms.

Chrysanthemum segetum
Corn marigold. An annual weed most frequently seen on arable land, rather than in meadows, but one that is relatively easy to naturalize in a loose sward, especially where the soil has recently been disturbed. The crown marigold (*C. coronaria*) is even lovelier, having flowers which are often rayed in two tones — lemon and dark yellow.

Knautia arvensis
Field scabious. A vigorous perennial with divided foliage and somewhat lax, branching stems which reach a height of 75–100cm (2ft 6in–3ft). It bears compound flowers with soft lilac-blue florets for much of the summer. A vigorous self-seeder but also easy to propagate from division. Rarely, a white form occurs.

Lythrum salicaria
Purple loosestrife. This plant is so-called because the flowers were thought to be insect-repellent, and were therefore tied in bunches to horses' bridles, in order to reduce the strife caused by flies. It is a clump-forming perennial with willow-like leaves and erect stems to around 1m (3ft), with narrow flowers spikes thickly clustered with vivid purple blooms in mid- to late summer. (N.B. Loosestrife is a noxious weed in some parts of North America, where it has been introduced.)

Origanum vulgare
Marjoram. The aromatic pot herb, lover of calcareous landscapes, is easy to establish in grassland as long as the soil is not too rich. Fragrant, heart-shaped basal leaves on a running rootstock form low domes until early summer, when the flower stems lengthen and are topped with lavender or pinkish-purple blooms which form a lively display. The pale colour of the flowers is set off by the dark, rusty green of the calyces. This is an excellent butterfly plant.

Typha latifolia
Reedmace — more widely known as the bullrush, though in fact it is not a rush at all. Mid-green, strap-like leaves develop through spring and summer, among which appear the stout flower-bearing stems that resemble dark brown clubs or maces with the texture of velvet. Commonly found growing in water, it is equally happy in moist meadow conditions where it prefers heavy soil to light sandy ones.

Marjoram (*Origanum vulgare*) is an aromatic herb commonly found on free-draining banks or pastures. Creeping mats of foliage hold their own against the grass.

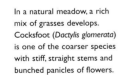

In a natural meadow, a rich mix of grasses develops. Cocksfoot (*Dactylis glomerata*) is one of the coarser species with stiff, straight stems and bunched panicles of flowers.

A BRONZE BORDER

▶ A member of the carrot family, *Bupleurum falcatum* has a quiet beauty, with greenish-yellow flowers during the summer period. It is a prolific producer of seed and easy to raise, sowing in spring in gritty compost and cool conditions. Though a rapid spreader, it is readily controlled.

▶ In the rich and subtle planting of this late-summer border, foliage hues are stronger than flower colours. The vivid purple of the dwarf berberis and the strong silver-grey of the grass are toned down by the soft greenish-yellow of bupleurum, kniphofia and lemon-coloured coreopsis. Catnip, diascias and a curiously pallid form of the evening primrose make up the complement of pastel flowers.

In a refreshing change from the riotous tones of summer, this small border makes a lively statement without the benefit of big flowers or primary colours. Small blooms are less likely to conflict with the foliage, used here to develop a fine cohesion and a disciplined colour range. The effect is of a Post-Impressionist *pointilliste* painting.

In high summer, this composition becomes so luxurious that it is hard to distinguish the basic outline plants. But all the essential elements of planting composition are here, from the framework shrubs and perennials to the infilling understorey of other herbaceous subjects. The berberis, for example, will retain its rounded profile during winter and, though they may lose their freshness of colour, the grasses and kniphofia also present a distinctive outline for autumn and winter. Continuity of interest is maintained with other perennials, like the pink and purple penstemons and the diascia, both of which flower continuously during the growing season, as well as by the changing foliage of the berberis as it deepens in colour through summer and into autumn.

In spite of strict colour control, the planting is relaxed and naturalistic – perfect for the garden's rural setting. Some of the species, particularly the yellow umbellifer, have been encouraged to self-seed, replicating themselves along the border; others have been planted to give a similar random effect. And, like a piece of natural landscape, changes here are gradual, since each plant has an extremely long flowering period.

▲ The grass, *Leymus arenarius*, makes a silvery contrast with bronze leaves as well as with the bright verbenas that complement the more sombre purples in the foliage hues of this border.

◄ Part of the charm of evening primrose is its somewhat bedraggled look. The gentle lemon colour of *Oenothera elata* subsp. *hookeri* is ephemeral, turning to apricot-orange as the flowers fade. Dark stems and foliage help to enhance the pale beauty of the flowers.

Ingredients

Key	Plant	Qty / Space (cm)	Substitute
①	*Anthemis tinctoria* 'E.C. Buxton'	1 /60	*Coreopsis verticillata* 'Moonbeam'
②	*Berberis thunbergii* 'Atropurpurea Nana'	1 /90	*B. t.* 'Bagatelle'
③	*Bupleurum falcatum*	>5 /60	*Foeniculum vulgare*
④	*Calamintha nepeta* ssp. *nepeta*	>5 /60	*Penstemon* 'Evelyn'
⑤	*Diascia* 'Lilac Belle'	>5 /45	*D. rigescens*
⑥	*Kniphofia* 'Green Jade'	1 /45	*Galtonia candicans*
⑦	*Leymus arenarius*	1 /60	*Helictotrichon sempervirens*
⑧	*Oenothera elata* ssp. *hookeri*	>3 /60	*Gaura lindheimeri*
⑨	*Penstemon* 'Burgundy'	3 /60	*Verbena corymbosa*
⑩	*Penstemon* 'Evelyn'	1 /60	*P.* 'Apple Blossom'
⑪	*Verbena rigida*	1 /45	*V.* x *hybrida*

Qty: *the number of specimens used in this recipe; numbers can be adjusted to suit a different site.*
Space: *recommended spacings for optimum growth (in centimetres).*

Groundwork: This kind of planting works best on good soil that has been deeply dug and dressed with compost or rotted manure. Many of the plants should spread out to fill their spaces quickly.

Planting procedure: The berberis will be quite small at planting time, so leave a 30cm (12in) gap all round it to discourage any neighbourly encroachment. The bupleurum has a loose, open habit and can be allowed to intertwine with the other plants, even to grow through them. Do not bother to support its lax stems, but let it find its own level. If it is happy, it will seed itself freely, creating a soft golden mist around the more solid colours of other plants.

Maintenance: Encourage plants to spread by gentle feeding during the growing season and by pulling bits of diascia or calamintha from the parent plants and replanting them. Diascias and penstemons are barely frost-hardy and they will need winter protection in cold areas. Alternatively, take cuttings of these perennials in late summer and overwinter them in a frost-free greenhouse, planting them out the following season when all risk of frost has passed.

An interesting range of perennials and low-growing shrubs, the penstemons are native to North and Central America. This wine-purple cultivar has the fitting name 'Burgundy'.

Green, waxy flowers, which turn yellowish-white only when aging, make *Kniphofia* 'Green Jade' a cool individual variety of red-hot poker.

✄ A large number of shrubs have bronze or purple foliage, but few colour up so well in autumn as *Berberis thunbergii* 'Atropurpurea'.

Planting Plan 5m x 2.5m (16ft x 8ft)

🐾 Bluest of the blue grasses, *Leymus arenarius* has a slowly creeping rootstock and will gradually spread to fill its allotted space. The modest flowers are the same shade of blue-grey as the leaves.

PLANT DIRECTORY

🐾 *Berberis thunbergii*
A highly variable shrub, as valuable for its foliage and outline as for its flower and fruits. *B. thunbergii* 'Atropurpurea Nana' is one of the most useful of the range of smaller, purple-leaved shrubs, forming low domes covered with simple, deep purple leaves whose colour intensifies to deep red in autumn. Small clusters of red-tinged yellow flowers appear in spring, to be followed in summer by small, shiny red berries.

🐾 *Bupleurum falcatum*
Sickle-leaved hare's ear. A European wildling in the carrot family with strange, single leaves pierced by the stems, and many-branched, somewhat lax flowering stems. The flowers, produced in loose umbels, are greenish-yellow. The plant's height depends on the fertility of the soil, and ranges from 30cm (12in) to about 75cm (2ft 6in).

🐾 *Calamintha grandiflora*
Catnip. An intensely aromatic member of the lavender and thyme family with small, creased nettle-like leaves, and purplish-pink trumpet flowers which, despite its name, are little more than 1cm (½in) long. A free-seeding perennial, in free-draining soil in a sunny position it is apt to become a nuisance.

🐾 *Diascia*
Twinspur. Spreading, mat-forming perennials from South Africa. Most diascias flower almost incessantly during the growing season and develop large drifts of colour from the network of underground roots. Tallest and handsomest is *D. rigescens*, with spires of shell-pink blooms. *D.* 'Lilac Belle' is lower-growing, but has a constant run of mauve flowers, each with a pair of tiny spurs at their backs.

🐾 *Leymus arenarius*
Bluest of the perennial grasses, this rhizomatous species can spread across a considerable area in a short time. The leaves grow up to 50cm (20in) in length and, at flowering, the plant may reach more than 1m (3ft). The leaf colour is bright blue-grey.

🐾 *Oenothera*
Evening primrose, so-called because some species are pollinated by night-flying insects and so produce their new flowers at night. Perennial species include *O. fruticosa*, which has such good garden forms as the bright yellow 'Fyrverkeri' (fireworks), and the trailing *O. macrocarpa*, whose large, pale yellow blooms are produced at ground level. The species illustrated here, like the common evening primrose (*O. biennis*), is either biennial or a short-lived perennial.

SPEEDY SHRUBS AND CLIMBERS

A judicious assembly of quick-growing shrubs brings colour, form and, above all, maturity to a relatively new garden. Sprawling shrub roses, a vigorous form of buddleja and a golden-leaved elder combine foliage and flower colour to make a spectacular flourish in this late-summer display, made even brighter with the clematis trained to drape its garlands over the foliage.

All these shrubs are fast-growing and will achieve the coverage shown – more than 2m (6ft) high and almost as wide – within three growing seasons. And yet they are easy to discipline, either by hard pruning in late winter or early spring, or by more gentle trimming, simply to keep them to size. Each has a lengthy lifespan but, because they are so

▶ *Rosa* 'Herbstfeuer' (syn. 'Autumn Fire') is a tall, vigorous variety which will grow more than 2m (6ft) in all directions. It concludes its long flowering season with a generous autumn flush.

▲ *Rosa glauca* is a large, spreading shrub rose grown as much for its intriguing blue-grey foliage, suffused with red, as for its small, single pink flowers. Mature specimens are generously furnished, in autumn, with hips that turn dark red as they age.

fast-developing, they can be considered as disposable, either to make room for other shrubs or to change the border's outline.

This is a bold planting, to be enjoyed from a distance as well as at close quarters. Almost all the constituents are framework plants but, together, they form a softened, gentle outline, full of subtleties of leaf and texture but richly decorated with flowers. The outline may lose its form a little in winter when the shrubs drop their leaves, but the inclusion of a variegated euonymus and winter- and spring-flowering daphnes, with the winter hips on the *Rosa glauca,* help to compensate. Plants at ground level, like *Viola cornuta*, supply a succession of quieter colour.

◄ The blue-green foliage of *Rosa glauca* contrasts dramatically with the gold of the *Sambucus racemosa* 'Aurea' and harmonizes with the silvery leaves of the buddleja. The flowers – mainly clematis and roses – are large and loud, making a joyous splash of crimson and purple, perfect against the golden or grey foliage. The aim is to create a strong summer climax, but each shrub has its own special off-season attributes: some of the roses bear hips as well as gorgeous blooms, and the foliage of both sambucus and *Rosa glauca* move through a fascinating pattern of changing hues from spring, when the young shoots are iridescent golden-green, to the end of the year, when purples and golds predominate.

Planting Plan   5m x 3m (16ft x 10ft)

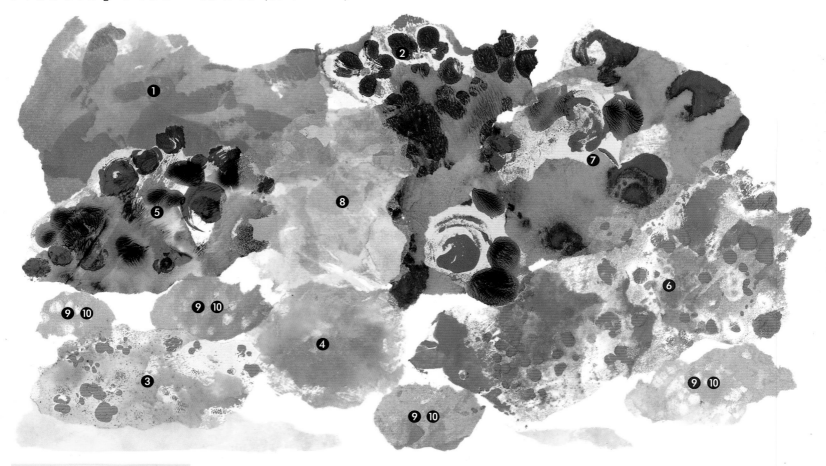

Ingredients

Key	Plant	Qty/Space (cm)	Substitute
①	*Buddleja davidii*	1 /250	*B.* 'Lochinch'
②	*Clematis* 'Jackmanii Superba'	1 /150	*C.* 'Perle d'Azur'
③	*Daphne burkwoodii* 'Variegata'	1 /100	*D. tangutica*
④	*Euonymus fortunei* 'Silver Queen'	1 /100	*E.* Emerald 'n' Gold
⑤	*Rosa* 'Charles de Mills'	1 /120	*R. gallica* 'Officinalis'
⑥	*Rosa glauca*	1 /150	*Indigofera heterantha*
⑦	*Rosa* 'Herbstfeuer'	1 /120	*R.* 'Danse du Feu'
⑧	*Sambucus racemosa* 'Aurea'	1 /150	*Physocarpus opulifolius* 'Dart's Gold'
⑨	*Viola cornuta* 'Alba'	>3 /25	*V.* 'Foxbrook Cream'
⑩	*Viola cornuta* 'Lilacina'	>3 /25	*V.* 'Maggie Mott'

Qty: *the number of specimens used in this recipe; numbers can be adjusted to suit a different site.*
Space: *recommended spacings for optimum growth (in centimetres).*

Notes: Ring the changes with the underplanting. A selection of perennial violas will give lasting delight, blooming from early spring through autumn. Dot these with bulbs – aconites for winter; miniature daffodils for spring; colchicums for autumn.

🍂 Golden elder (*Sambucus racemosa* 'Aurea') is seen in vivid and startling contrast to the deep purple-blue flowers of *Clematis* 'Jackmanii Superba'.

Horned violets (*Viola cornuta*) can be encouraged to spread themselves around shrubs like this daphne, filling gaps and flowering away for much of the year.

▲ In this harmonious colour mix, the hues of clematis, rose and elder – purple, red and gold – are all replicated, in more subtle suffusions, in the blue-grey foliage of *Rosa glauca*.

Groundwork: Shrubs are mostly self-sufficient, once established, but rapid-growers like these will be hungry, especially when first put in, and should be planted into very well prepared ground. Deep digging, with generous dressings of rotted manure, will help to ensure they get off to a good start. Where the natural soil is poor or stony, a slow-release plant food such as bonemeal should also be added to the planting hole.

Planting procedure: With containerized shrubs, this planting can be made at any time of year, but the ideal season for planting shrubs is autumn, after they have become naturally dormant but before soil temperatures drop to the levels where root development no longer take place. Space the larger shrubs – roses, elder and buddleja – a minimum of 1.5m (5ft) apart. Add a handful of bonemeal to each planting hole and heel the plants in well. If your garden is exposed or windy, use a stout stake to secure the shrubs for their first few seasons.

The ground-covering perennials are all natural spreaders, but you will achieve a

❧ Though grown mainly for its foliage, and for its crop of autumn hips, *Rosa glauca* produces small, single pink flowers which have their own simple charm.

quicker cover if you divide them at least once during their first season. *Viola cornuta* plants can even be split down into single stems, each with a little shock of roots, and replanted 20–30cm (8–12in) apart.

Maintenance: Such rapid-growing shrubs as elder and buddleja will respond to hard pruning by producing vigorous young shoots furnished with large, lush foliage. Late winter is the best time to prune, just before the buds begin to swell. Take out all leggy or overgrown branches; cut back the remainder to the base of the plant or to a plump bud.

Roses which flower once only and spring-flowering shrubs need a different regime: prune these immediately after flowering unless they produce a berry or hip crop. The clematis garlands will also need to be cut back from the host plant in winter.

Future: Rapid-growing shrubs give speedy results and a decade or more of service. However, the inclusion of some medium- to longer-term shrubs could enhance the display. A decorative holly or, on the right soil, a camellia or two would ensure winter delight, especially if accompanied by the winter-flowering honeysuckle, *Lonicera fragrantissima*. At ground level, beef up the low-growing perennials with spring bulbs and plug any gaps with summer annuals.

❧ When choosing clematis to grow through host shrubs, select varieties which flower after the longest day, as these can be pruned hard in late winter, allowing the shrubs to be pruned too.

Buddleja davidii, in all its varieties, is irresistible to butterflies. To encourage a late-summer crop of the nectar-rich flowers, try pruning this rapid-growing shrub hard in late spring.

PLANT DIRECTORY

❧ *Clematis* 'Jackmanii'
One of the earliest of the large-flowered hybrids to be raised, this clematis is also one of the most foolproof. Four-sepalled flowers in a rich royal blue are produced on the current season's growth. 'Jackmanii Superba' has even larger, purple blooms and 'Jackmanii Alba' produces a sparing crop of bluish-white, semi-double flowers on the previous season's wood, before the late-summer flush of single blooms. Prune single-flowered forms hard in late winter.

❧ *Daphne* x *burkwoodii*
A semi-evergreen daphne growing to 1.5m (5ft) in good soil, with narrow, simple leaves and intensely fragrant, pale pink flowers, produced in a main flush during early spring, but with sporadic blooms borne throughout summer. Not especially long-lived, but a perfect small shrub and easy to replace either by layering or by taking cuttings.

❧ *Euonymus fortunei*
Evergreen species of spindleberry with its small, simple leaves carried on trailing stems. The flowers are insignificant but many varieties have been developed with attractive foliage colour. Variegated forms are particularly useful for providing mats of weedproof winter cover. Gold-leaved forms include Emerald 'n' Gold, whose young buds are gold, making a contrast with the darker green mature foliage.

❧ *Rosa gallica*
Group of old-fashioned roses, grown since medieval times, whose buds are rounded rather than pointed and whose open blooms display tight arrangements of petals, often characteristically quartered. Richly fragrant and coming in colours which vary from the deep wine-red of *R. gallica* 'Officinalis' – the red rose of Lancaster – to the striated two-tone pink of the equally ancient 'Rosa Mundi'. Gallica roses have but one flowering season – in early to midsummer – and should then be pruned only if necessary, immediately after flowering.

❧ *Rosa glauca*
An engaging wild rose species, as valuable for its foliage colour as for the flowers and fruits. The young shoots and leaf tips are coppery pink but, as the pinnate leaves mature, this colour changes to a rich pewter-like blue-grey. The single, five-petalled pink flowers are small and undramatic but have a simple appeal. The hips, which develop in early autumn, are maroon. Though easy to raise from seed, this is a variable species and it is worth sowing a batch to select seedlings with the best foliage colour.

❧ *Sambucus racemosa* 'Aurea'
A European elder whose leaves are handsomely toothed and, in the form 'Aurea', suffused with gold. Umbels of off-white flowers, produced in early summer, are unexciting but, if allowed to mature, red berries may be formed. If grown in full sun the foliage may scorch, but in dappled shade the leaf colour runs through a sequence of yellow-greens. Prune hard to ensure vigorous young growths.

▶ Bright blue nigellas, drumstick garlics and magenta *Gladiolus byzantinus* brighten an annual border in early summer, but in autumn seedheads of the same plants, even when fully spent, provide almost as fine a display, just waiting to be garnished with hoarfrost.

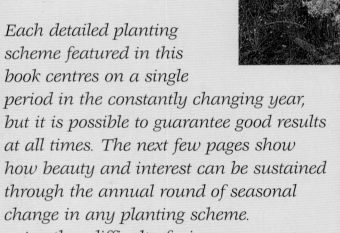

Each detailed planting scheme featured in this book centres on a single period in the constantly changing year, but it is possible to guarantee good results at all times. The next few pages show how beauty and interest can be sustained through the annual round of seasonal change in any planting scheme.

Another difficulty facing many gardeners is a so-called problem site, or even sites. Rather than being viewed as problematic, the conditions prevailing in such sites are so different from the norm that they simply need a special approach. Once the right choice of plants has been made, the results will not only be as pleasing as those on more favoured sites – they could be even better. The concluding pages of this section visit some of the more commonly encountered situations.

Glory

at all times

Colours in this border have drained away during the autumn, leaving behind distinctive shapes of such perennials as *Sedum spectabile*. Now, grey frost paints yet another garden picture, neither loud nor dramatic, but with a quiet beauty.

SEASONAL CHANGE

However well planted a garden may be, it cannot sustain its summer climax for the whole year, but there are ways to increase interest and enhance seasonal beauty as the garden travels through a series of moods, each varying in intensity. Winter is low-key, a process of purification which ends as the first frail flowers emerge. Spring begins hesitantly, but growth accelerates up to the longest day, then summer sees increasing blowsiness as fading flowers begin to outnumber fresh buds. The decline of the year has its own special appeal as new colours emerge from altering foliage, ripening berries and surprising autumn beauties. This constant change is what makes the art of gardening so absorbing.

Spring promise

Emerging and developing plants generate an abundance of fresh background foliage, which provides the bulk of spring vegetation as well as much of the form and enables the gardener to concentrate on maximizing flower power.

Spring colour can be increased by adding as many early flowers as possible, virtually all of which are planted in the previous autumn, sometimes to replace short-term summer plants. Wallflowers, forget-me-nots or winter pansies can be used this way. Less common spring-flowering biennials or perennials might include double daisies, drumstick primulas, arabis and, for late spring to early summer colour, Canterbury bells.

A blossom-bearing tree brings short-term drama to the outline, which is heightened if some of the shrubs also bear spring flowers. Ornamental apples, cherries and hawthorns make brilliant spring displays and most have attractive shapes for other times of year. On acid soils, massing rhododendrons will make a spectacular display. For limy or chalky soils, a gorgeous choice includes early flowering currants, such as the sweet-scented, yellow *Ribes odoratum*, amelanchiers with their frail

▶ **Late winter melts into spring in this semi-shaded setting. Oriental hybrid hellebores (*Helleborus orientalis*), just in the process of setting seed, still provide beauty as their flowers turn green. North American phloxes, selected forms of *P. stolonifera*, create a lavender-blue drift, which is complemented by the Asian azaleas in the background.**

◄ Members of the onion tribe (*Allium*) have flowers in clusters at the tips of their long, smooth stems. The majority bloom from mid-spring to early summer, varying in size and height from a few centimetres to more than a metre. This mid-season species, *Allium caeruleum*, is unusual for its clear blue flower colour.

white flowers, lilacs in all kinds of hues and, later, deliciously scented mock oranges.

At ground level, bulbs are the biggest providers of spring delight. Grape hyacinths, crocuses, anemones, scillas and chionodoxas can be littered among emerging understorey plants to bloom early, before other plants engulf them. Later, narcissus become the most dominant genus, from delicate little alpine species such as N. cyclamineus to monster hybrids like N. 'King Alfred' or the bold, ruffled lemon cups of N. 'Ice Follies'. The latter look best from a distance, but they do not naturalize in grass or woodland half so comfortably as do such smaller, more dainty hybrids as N. 'Peeping Tom' or N. 'Jack Snipe', both of which have prettily reflexed petals.

Tulips take over from narcissus. Colours can be as bright and bold or as gentle and understated as you like. *Tulipa viridiflora* varieties such as green and pink 'Groenland' or green and white 'Spring Green' blend seamlessly into subtle colour schemes. For a jolly, vivid red choose T. 'Apeldoorn', or for dazzling yellow, 'Golden Apeldoorn'.

Bulbs contribute little in the way of fancy foliage, therefore blending them with spring-flowering herbaceous species can improve the display, especially if plants are selected for leaf as well as flower. White-flowered variegated honesty, a startling explosion of green and white, teams well with cream or white tulips. Spring peas (*Lathyrus vernus*) come in several shades including magenta, pale pink and pure blue. Doronicums are golden and dependable, but not as exciting as *Thermopsis montana*, which combines dark green, three-lobed leaves with cheerful yellow flower spikes.

Young foliage makes an effective spring backing. Many roses and almost all herbaceous paeonies have coppery or bronze leaves and stems when they first emerge, which make a pleasing foil for yellow or golden flowers. The greenness of developing summer and autumn perennials can be enhanced by including one or two good foliage plants, such as gold-leaved *Valeriana phu* 'Aurea' or dark-leaved perennials like *Cimicifuga simplex* 'Brunette'. These, along with the remaining understorey plants, will help to ease the transition from spring to summer and, as they develop, will help to disguise the dying leaves of the spring bulbs.

▲ Tulips bring a dramatic burst of colour in mid-spring, whether they are used in formal bedding or informally. Here, the lily-flowered variety, *Tulipa* 'West Point', highlights a corner planted with quieter blooms such as white-flowered sweet cicely (*Myrrhis odorata*) and green *Euphorbia characias*.

Summer beauty

▼ In an early summer display in cool blues and clinical white, delphiniums in the Blue Jade Group make a strong contrast with the 2m (6ft) sprays of white-flowered *Crambe cordifolia*. The crambe flowers once, but delphiniums can be encouraged to stage a reprise if they are cut back and fed before they set seed.

Plantings that are designed to be at their peak in spring, such as Spring Palette (pages 108–111) and A Woodland Scene (pages 112–115), need extra plants to carry them through the summer months. When such spring plants as tulips, forget-me-nots and wallflowers have faded, summer flowers will be needed to replace them in the same spot. A good spring border can carry plenty of perennials for later flowering, but can also be furnished with summer-flowering species that obligingly disappear below ground when not in bloom. Agapanthus, galtonias, tigridias, gladioli and other summer-flowering bulbs help the late display and are lovely if accompanied by the dark chocolate cosmos and those dahlias selected for border use, such as *D.* 'Preston Park' or 'Bishop of Llandaff'. In early spring, all these plants are either still out of sight underground or yet to be planted.

Climbing plants, set to scale some of the early flowering trees and shrubs, will provide later colour, be they such clematis as *C. viticella*, or perennial peas such as *Lathyrus tingitanus* and *L. latifolius*. Be selective when choosing these climbers, using only those that can be cut hard

Valuable herbaceous climbers

▼

Cobaea scandens

Eccremocarpus scaber

Ipomoea caerulea

Ipomoea lobata

Lathyrus odoratus

Lathyrus rotundifolius

Lophospermum erubescens

Maurandya barclayana

Rhodochiton atropurpureum

Tropaeolum peregrinum

back in autumn to ensure that the spring display of their host trees and shrubs remains unspoilt.

As long as there are enough left behind to spread seeds, some of the spring biennials can be removed after flowering to make room for new introductions. Thus, a spring border, if it is well lit and on good soil, can be transformed into a collection of tender summer perennials. Most of the plants in A Taste of the Tropics (pages 68–71), for example, have been introduced purely for the summer season and, being tender, will be lifted in the autumn and transferred to a frost-free place.

Another way to extend the life of a spring border is to introduce hardy summer annuals. For example, mignonette or night-scented stock, though less than conspicuous, should be encouraged to seed everywhere for their delicious fragrance rather than their looks. They will blend with more showy annuals such as nigellas, clarkias and, in hot displays, nasturtiums. The latter are perennial and will root from cuttings, but they are easily grown as direct-sown annuals. Some, such as *Tropaeolum majus* 'Apricot Twist' and 'Hermine Grasshoff', have long-lasting, double flowers.

▲ In midsummer, when days are bright and light levels high, the most unlikely colours can harmonize. Here, pink opium poppies (*Papaver somniferum*) associate with a dusky salmon-orange day lily (*Hemerocallis*). The glaucous foliage of the poppies makes a neutral background hue that blends the other colours.

▶ Two clematis make a delightful alternative to roses or honeysuckle around a cottage door in high summer, when climbers and wall plants reach their climax of growth. The blue *Clematis* 'Perle d'Azur' is at its best; the yellow *C. tangutica* is just beginning to flower. From summer's end, the fluffy seedheads will make a second display.

Autumn richness

▲ Flaming tints appear among the russets and browns on a large number of trees and shrubs in autumn, but few stage such a brilliant display as the ornamental vine (*Vitis coignetiae*). Here, the display is more spectacular at the close of the season, with the vine contrasting with the golden yellow leaves of the climbing *Hydrangea anomala* ssp. *petiolaris*, than it was in high summer.

Even in the most groomed gardens, the autumn scene generally tends to be one of dishevelment. Fortunately, there is no great problem with that. Leaf litter is both a normal part of the yearly cycle and acceptable, and it can look attractive when lit up by slanting afternoon sunshine. Shrewd planting, though, will help to introduce some quality colour and form to the declining garden.

Resist the temptation to tidy things up. Fallen and fading foliage can look almost as alluring as flowers, especially when it forms colourful carpets beneath the shrubs and trees on which it has grown. If the weather is calm, you can expect pools of red below maples, orange below cherries and sharp yellow beneath ornamental birches.

Certain plants are unable to flower until shortening autumn days stimulate their buds to develop and open. Thus, asters, chrysanthemums, some salvia species, *Lobelia laxiflora*, toad lilies and a host of other perennials will look their best close to the autumnal equinox. In a mixed planting, it is worth including a generous sprinkling of these simply to extend the summer season, but if there is the space, it is worth considering having an exclusively autumnal border, or at least some part of the garden set aside for a special autumn flourish.

Many bulbs are useful at this time of the year. The naked flower spikes of such autumn beauties as colchicums, *Amaryllis belladonna* and the autumn-flowering crocuses suddenly erupt directly from the ground, before there is any sign of leaf.

Few trees bloom in autumn, though some *Eucryphia* species might carry flowers until the equinox, but there are plenty of colourful berries. The careful choice of spring-blossom trees can provide an autumn bonus. Mountain ashes, or rowans, especially the Himalayan ones, have pleasant blossom and good foliage, but at this time of year their fruits are nothing short of magnificent, ranging in hue from the pure white of *Sorbus cashmiriana* through the pinks of *S.* × *vilmorinii* and *S. hupehensis* to the bright red of *S.* × *kewensis*.

As days shorten and nights grow colder, shelter for wildlife becomes more important, making it important to resist the temptation

Fresh autumn tints

The flask-shaped hips of *Rosa moyesii* contrast handsomely here, not only with its own foliage turning yellow, but with the sombre purple leaves of a smokebush (*Cotinus coggygria* 'Royal Purple').

Plants' special needs

Both shrubs are easy to grow, happy in virtually any soil and benefit from an occasional hard pruning, taking out all old wood, almost to ground level. When the shrubs grow into one another, it is important to maintain a balance, making sure that neither swamps its neighbour.

Others to try

In dry, alkaline soil, the red-leaved filbert (*Corylus maxima* 'Purpurea') gives a similar effect to the smokebush and, if unchecked, would grow big enough to allow the vigorous *Rosa* 'Scharlachglut' (syn. 'Scarlet Fire') to pleach through its stems. As well as producing long garlands of single, scarlet blooms, this rose bears a heavy crop of orange hips.

Off-season echoes

The shrubs provide their own off-season displays: in late spring, the rose is covered with pink or blood-red, single blooms and the smokebush, besides running through a range of dark foliage hues, develops loose panicles of tiny flowers which slowly develop into fluffy seedheads which look rather like puffs of smoke.

▲ Red rose hips of *Rosa moyesii* with dark smokebush (*Cotinus coggygria* 'Royal Purple') foliage.

◄ The intense scarlet foliage of oriental maples in autumn can be brighter and more cheerful than a whole bed full of summer flowers. Conditions must be right for such a transformation – chilly nights followed by hot, sunny days – and the choice of species is also important. Here, *Acer japonicum* makes a fiery contrast with the dark yew hedge.

to cut everything back. Unless you need to prepare the way for tiny spring bulbs or late winter plants, postpone the annual clean-up until spring, but bear in mind, too, that this is the best time for planting bulbs, trees, shrubs and a great many perennials. Also, if you are carrying out major overhauls to any part of your garden, it may be difficult for you to leave adequate wildlife cover.

Winter delight

In a cold climate, forays into the garden are likely to be at their briefest during winter, so riotous displays are unnecessary. With that in mind, and assuming a well-mixed planting, effecting at least a degree of winter continuity in a planting could hardly be easier. All that is needed is an occasional plant, or plant group, in both outline and understorey sections that will give a little off-season joy, or perhaps nothing more than some winter fragrance.

There should be a winter primrose or two, some winter-flowering honeysuckle (*Lonicera fragrantissima*) and perhaps winter cherry

(*Prunus × subhirtella* 'Autumnalis'). Sometimes hellebores come into bloom, but there is always winter jasmine (*Jasminum nudiflorum*), so generous with its clean yellow blooms, each one perfectly set off by the green stems. As soon as the days begin to lengthen, these stalwart few will be joined by an increasing trickle of emerging blooms.

Evergreens help enormously, retaining an element of life and freshness in the winter garden, but making a dark, lustrous backdrop in summer. Those that provide winter flower or fragrance are to be doubly valued. All the

▶ Winter twigs glow in the sunlight. A number of shrubs lend themselves to coppicing – that is, being cut hard back every spring to produce sheaves of young stems which develop bright colours. Willow, the bramble *Rubus cockburnianus* and the dogwood *Cornus alba* 'Sibirica' have all been used here to create an especially colourful mixture.

▶ When winter begins to move into spring, weather can be fickle. Warm days can lure forth such early beauties as the snakeshead fritillary (*Fritillaria meleagris*), which may then be shocked by a snowfall. Luckily, such rugged species are unharmed by a brief cold snap and continue to bloom, even when surrounded by a winter scene.

camellias are handsome, but members of the *C. × williamsii* group carry a premium because many of them provide sporadic blooms in winter as well as finishing with a spring flush. Sarcococca is a humble suckering shrub that goes almost unnoticed in summer, except that its small evergreen leaves are pleasantly glossy. However, the sweet, honey fragrance of its tiny tufty flowers make it an essential plant for the winter garden.

Hellebores slowly start coming into bloom around the shortest day and keep the form and beauty of their flowers right through to spring. Oriental hellebore hybrids are the most dependable. These arise from a mix of closely related species including *Helleborus orientalis*, *H. multifidus*, *H. torquatus* and *H. odorus*, and occur in a range of subdued colours from pure white through pinks and purples to a deep, brooding, midnight purple-black. Some have spotting, streaking or stippling in their sepals. Their one fault is modesty: the flowers are inclined to hang their heads so that you have to turn them up to gaze into them. In a border planted with tall summer perennials, be sure to include a couple of the big Corsican hellebores (*H. argutifolius*), since these are bushy and evergreen with distinctive foliage and apple-green flowers, produced in sprays, which last for months.

As winter draws to a close, but long before leaves emerge on trees and shrubs, buds and twigs will change in colour with the rising sap and day by day the whole outline planting will run through a series of subtle changes. You can accentuate these by including outline plants that carry either catkins, such as the common alder (*Alnus glutinosus*) and hazel (*Corylus avellana*), or handsome winter buds, such as *Aesculus indica*. Most of the willows produce lustrous silvery catkins in late winter, whereas alders, hazels and evergreen *Garrya elliptica* have delightful tassles which lengthen as they mature through winter into spring, provided a male form has been selected.

Keeping the winter outline

◀ **Globe thistles (*Echinops ritro*) against the purple foliage of *Berberis thunbergii* f. *atropurpurea*.**

Even in death, the outline of the globe thistle has a gaunt beauty, especially when set against the dark purple backdrop of *Berberis thunbergii* f. *atropurpurea*.

Plants' special needs

Such rugged plants as these are happy in any soil, but in rich, fertile types the thistle will grow almost to 2m (6ft) and flower more spectacularly. Eventually, the dead stems become untidy and will need clearing away before the end of winter. This berberis has been trimmed into an informal hedge, probably with an annual clipping which keeps it looking young and leafy.

Others to try

The green-leaved forms of berberis are as delightful as this sombre purple one. An alternative might be *B. darwinii* or *B. × stenophylla* 'Corallina', both of which have coppery-orange or yellow flowers. In summer, the giant scabious (*Cephalaria gigantea*) would make a striking contrast as a foreground plant, since its flowers are pale creamy yellow.

Off-season echoes

This is an all-season planting, but against the emerging purple foliage you could try the lovely yellow, lily-flowered tulip hybrid, *Tulipa* 'West Point'.

PROBLEM SITUATIONS

Apoor gardener's problem is an inspired gardener's special planting opportunity. That sounds rather pat, of course, but there is nothing like a spot of adversity to bring out the best in a plant-lover. Every garden has at least one problem area, and in some localities the whole plot might prove daunting. But since there is an excellent choice of plants for almost every type of ground, however harsh the conditions, it should be possible to create a fine garden anywhere, even in a hostile environment. On the following pages, some of the more commonly encountered garden challenges are discussed and suggestions made for turning every one of them into a colourful success.

Town gardens and walls

◄ In a crowded space, careful selection is essential and every plant must pay its rent. In this tiny town garden most of the character comes from foliage – a mix that varies widely in both texture and shape. There are few flowers, but those that have been permitted provide gentle relief from the green.

A town garden, even one with the narrowest and most cramped dimensions, can be utterly charming if it is well designed and, more importantly, carefully planted.

Maintaining an interesting outline that is full of character is all important, but in a small space this may involve constant adjustment and occasional ruthlessness. Trees and shrubs may have to be removed long before they become too large, and invasive plants may have to be controlled. Scale (pages 40–41), as well as the ultimate size and spread of each plant, must be given careful consideration. There is no harm in introducing species that will outgrow their allotted space, since many of them can be so beautiful, but you must expel them when they grow too large, or you will seriously damage the planting balance.

The size of some plants can be controlled by root pruning, containerization or strategic pruning and training, in extreme cases along the lines of bonsai or penn jing. An advantage of growing certain trees and shrubs in containers, which by constricting the roots results in smaller growth, is that the plants are sometimes pushed into maturity at a smaller size than if they were growing in open ground. Some plants lend themselves more readily to this than others. Magnolias, for instance, do not respond well to root pruning, but some of the smaller species, such as *M. stellata*, do well in containers. Magnolias always grow the wrong way when pruned, but privet, hawthorns, hollies, laurels (especially Portuguese laurel) and box can be bullied as much as you like. Although some shrub roses can be kept to size, it is wise to select those with moderate vigour, and essential to choose either repeat-flowering kinds, or those that produce good crops of autumn hips.

Containers are excellent for small gardens because they provide a series of extra planting opportunities. This is especially useful where ground is paved or concreted, but cunningly sited containers can also transform a difficult corner or a spot that calls for a special focal point, such as opposite a window. Once in position, containers can be as permanently planted as borders with such compact shrubs as hebes, daphnes, dwarf conifers or heathers, or they can be used to present a succession of displays: winter and spring bulbs followed by

◀ A crowded roof garden burgeons with masses of foliage in a huge selection of shapes and colours. Despite the restricted space, such large-growing and potentially invasive species as bamboos and the huge grass *Arundo donax* have been used to excellent effect.

▶ Well-chosen containerized plants bring a tiny paved area to life. Bold-leaved hosta, cerise-flowered achimenes, lilies and pelargoniums provide a temporary display, supported by evergreen rhododendrons, camellias and climbing hydrangeas.

summer flowers – perhaps fuchsias or trailing pelargoniums – with plenty of cascading spray chrysanthemums for autumn.

Most gardens have vertical planting space – walls, fences, pillars – but in very small plots, there may be more vertical surfaces to furnish than horizontal ones. From the simple trick of twining a rambling rose up into the branches of an old apple tree, to composing a timed planting plan for a length of wall, upright gardening offers some of the richest planting opportunities. The same principles as in horizontal gardening apply, with outline planting taking the form of such plants as Japanese quinces (*Chaenomeles*) or winter-sweet (*Chimonanthus praecox*). These retain their shape all year round, even when trained hard to the wall surface, and make a frame-work through which such infill plants as late summer-flowering clematis or herbaceous climbers as sweet peas or morning glories can be threaded. Where conditions allow, a couple of show-stoppers could be included: in warm areas, a climbing lily like bomarea or gloriosa perhaps, or, in cooler, more moist conditions, the ravishing waxy-flowered *Lapageria rosea*.

Though they give shelter from the worst of the weather, walls can cause nasty wind eddies in a small garden, which sometimes rip climbers away from their supports. Take care, therefore, to select robust wall plants, and to anchor them well before training more delicate climbers through their branches. Japanese quinces are excellent for this, having constitutions so rugged that they will bloom through frost, will survive hurricanes with minimal damage, yet bear delectable winter blossom and big, edible fruits in late summer. Walls can also create dry shade areas; for planting ideas for such areas see Planting in Dry Shade (pages 148–149).

The limited dimensions of a town or small walled garden make it even more imperative to choose only the absolute best plants. Each one, even a tiny alpine, will take up a much bigger proportion of the total area than in a large garden, and therefore must pay its rent. Never accept an inferior plant, unless it has special sentimental value, and never tolerate a plant that will not thrive. I give plants two chances: if a chosen one dies, I replace it, if the second plant dies, I find something better.

Water and bog gardens

◄ The tranquillity of still water is enhanced by relaxed, informal planting. Lily leaves float undisturbed on the surface, shading the water and breaking up reflected images; such waterside plants as yellow iris give brief displays, but the bulk of the beauty here comes from the lush foliage of sedges, grasses and rushes.

A natural water course or low-lying ground that naturally holds water provides ideal conditions for a water or bog garden and so should never be seen as a disadvantage. But in the vast majority of gardens, installing a water feature will require the construction of a pond and a piped water supply. Man-made water features seldom have the advantages of damp surroundings, so it may be necessary to make an artificial bog by excavating soil, laying a waterproof membrane and replacing soil over it. Alternatively, a lush, waterside effect can be created by using plants that resemble wetland species but which grow in normal soil.

Genuine wetland plants grow vigorously and expand rapidly, soon developing a thick mass of vegetation which will often grow very tall in summer. This habit must be borne in mind when siting the plants, the tallest and most vigorous being positioned at the rear, or at least in places where they will not obscure too much of the view. Furthermore, the spring flowers of some wetland species, such as *Darmera peltata* and the bold arum relative lysichiton, are considerably smaller than the huge leaves that follow. Such plants seldom look happy where space is restricted, and where the water feature is limited in size it is better to scale down the planting, selecting smaller marsh plants such as *Caltha palustris*, the soft lilac double cuckoo flower (*Cardamine pratensis* 'Flore Pleno') and the gorgeous range of lesser celandines (*Ranunculus ficaria*). Among these, the variety 'Brazen Hussy' has dark bronze leaves, and there are double and single flowers in colours from greenish-white, through yellows to a deep coppery orange.

For early summer delight, collect Asiatic primulas, not only candelabra kinds, such as *P. japonica* and *P. pulverulenta*, but smaller beauties such as the delicate, nodding *P. alpicola*, spring-flowering *P. rosea* and *P. vialii*. The rat-tail flower spikes of the latter are crimson in bud, opening to an extraordinary contrasting shade of pale lilac-mauve. Although the plant is short-lived, it is easy to raise from seed.

On dry soil, non-wetland plants with big bold foliage help to create a spurious wetland look. Some, such as ligularias, are as happy in rich but relatively well-drained soil as in a bog. Others, like the huge-leaved *Rheum palmatum* or even taller angelica, grow well on normal soil as long as it does not dry out or bake hard. Hostas, traditionally grown near water, are happy in normal soil too, and may be less susceptible to slug and snail damage if their habitat is not too moist. Their solid leaves complement the feathery foliage of ferns, all of which look natural growing near water and many of which will tolerate dry soil as long as it is not in strong sunshine; aspleniums, dryopteris and polystichums are all in this last category. Tulips also work well (see By the Water's Edge, pages 98–101).

Outline, especially off-season outline, is as important in waterside planting as anywhere else. Trees with branches arching or weeping over the water can be doubly attractive when their image is reflected in the surface. On a

scaled-down pond, dwarf Japanese maples are excellent for this, as are some of the small, pendulous willows such as *Salix purpurea* 'Nancy Saunders', or possibly *S. caprea* 'Kilmarnock'. Resist the temptation, though, of planting larger weeping willows since these will grow huge and have damaging roots.

◀ *Primula bulleyana* with white arum (*Zantedeschia aethiopica*).

The hot colours of *Primula bulleyana* seedlings, one of the Asiatic primulas, dominate a superbly planted bog garden. Southern African arums and dark, velvety *Iris chrysographes* add exotic highlights. Water forget-me-nots provide contrasting blue dots.

Plants' special needs

Make sure that perennial weeds are absent before planting, and encourage the plants to seed until a self-replicating colony has developed. Where moisture is plentiful, feeding anything more than a very light spring dressing of manure or compound fertilizer usually results in plants growing too lush and flowers being relatively small.

Others to try

Giant cowslips (*Primula florindae* and *P. sikkimensis*) have yellow or golden flowers, but *P. florindae* bears an exquisite fragrance, stronger than that of European cowslips. Tall-growing globe flowers such as *Trollius chinensis* would also blend in well here, perhaps with Siberian irises (*Iris sibirica*), whose tall stems of blue flowers are followed by tan seed capsules.

Off-season echoes

Bog gardens tend to look their best in spring and early summer. *Primula bulleyana* will not bloom for long after the longest day, but using rodgersias as foliage plants helps, because many produce late summer blooms. For later in autumn, try the feathery purple blooms of vernonia.

◀ **Drumstick primulas** (*Primula denticulata*) produce tall flower stems at roughly the same time as tulips. Though technically perennials, they tend to be short-lived and should therefore be propagated from seed regularly.

A water-saving garden

Drought-resistant plants

As water becomes an increasingly sought-after commodity, many areas have restrictions on the amount available for gardening. As a result, the need for water-thrifty gardens is expanding. A clever combination of drought-tolerant plants and water-saving practices will create a garden that requires minimal or even no additional water during extended bouts of dry weather or drought.

Limiting your plant choice to species that thrive in dry conditions need not seriously restrict your choices, since a vast number of plants come from the semi-arid regions of the world. Indeed, some of our richest and most beautiful floras are to be found in such dry regions of the world as Southern Africa, the Mediterranean and the deserts of North, Central and South America.

The choice of outline plants for a drought-resistant garden is hardly more restricting than for any other kind. Once trees have become established, most are deep rooted enough to search out their own moisture. Pea family members such as gleditsias, robinias, laburnums and sophoras can be especially drought-resistant. In mild regions, evergreen *Pittosporum tobira* produces intensely fragrant, creamy blossoms in spring and summer.

Cherries and crab apples seem to dislike too dry a climate, but hawthorns are tougher and develop into pleasingly rounded trees. The Afghan native, *Crataegus tanacetifolia*, is a moderate- to slow-growing tree with creamy blossom in early summer and pea-sized orange fruits in autumn. Such Mediterranean species as figs, almonds, Corsican pines and Judas trees (*Cercis siliquastrum*) all make characterful outline trees, some more handsome in leaf than in flower. The decorative value of such Australian species as *Eucalyptus gunnii* cannot be denied, though in many parts of the world they have become troublesome aliens.

Artemisia 'Powis Castle'

Cistus ladanifer

Dianthus deltoides

Helichrysum splendidum

Lavandula stoechas

London Pride (Saxifraga × urbium)

Primula auricula

Rosmarinus officinalis

Sedum spathulifolium 'Cape Blanco'

◀ Colourful herbaceous plants, including opium poppies, catmint, stachys and euphorbias help to create a luxuriant effect, in spite of a chronic shortage of water. This dry, gravel garden is in an area where rainfall is low, that is less than 53cm (23in), and the soil is very sharp-draining.

◀ Rocks, cacti and succulents are used to create architectural shapes in a simple, subtropical garden. In an arid climate, such plants can be used to make a garden which is as interesting as one in a high rainfall area, but here, the desert effect is relieved by the greenness of the artificially watered lawn.

◀ Planted among stachys, sedums and cotton lavender, garlics (*Allium*) provide a colourful overture to the later summer display. Most garlics thrive on minimal rainfall, flowering profusely, even though their lower foliage often dies away before the blooms themselves have fully opened.

Among drought-tolerant shrubs, there is a predominance of silver and grey foliage. Helichrysums, lavender, rosemary, Jerusalem sage (*Phlomis*) and many of the wormwoods (*Artemisia*) sport handsome grey-green leaves. The more conspicuous of the rock roses are darker green, sometimes with glutinous foliage, making them excellent companions to contrast with the grey, and have the added attraction of large, bright pink or white flowers. Here, too, the pea family is well represented, with such beauties as Mount Etna broom (*Genista aetnensis*), which is shrouded with a golden mist of flowers and can be grown into a small tree. The dark blue-green Portuguese laurel (*Prunus lusitanica*) copes with drought, often flowering more profusely than in lush conditions, and can be grown naturally or used for topiary.

Drought-proof infill, or understorey, plants are also plentiful - ground-covering succulents like sedums, cotyledons, some of the mat-forming pinks, sun roses (*Helianthemum*), herbs like marjoram, sage and thyme and mulleins, which make rosettes of moisture-conserving foliage in the year before they bloom. Drought-loving euphorbias, especially *E. characias,* will seed about, developing self-expanding colonies that give winter interest as well as cool summer greenness. The grape vine (*Vitis vinifera*) must also be included.

In addition to the shrewd choice of plants, some basic water-conservation measures in the garden will ensure that whatever water is available is used to maximum benefit. Bare soil between plants looks ugly and increases evaporation rates. Laying thick organic mulches on the soil surface, as well as ensuring the fastest possible ground cover, will conserve the soil's moisture content. The soil itself must be in excellent heart, with a fine, crumbly texture and high organic content.

Create shade with tall plants, shrubs and trees. These will help to cool some of the ground, reducing evaporation, and allow for a richer variation of plants as well as moods and styles within the garden. If you do have to water, do so thoroughly, at night, and water to soak, not to sprinkle. This will increase the length of the intervals between waterings.

Planting in dry shade

The combination of dry soil and shade is one of the most commonly encountered problem situations in gardens, especially in urban settings, where high buildings, walls and trees can block the sun all day long and throw a planting area into almost permanent gloom. Nonetheless, even in this most challenging of sites there are exciting possibilities.

Foliage needs to work far harder in such conditions, and variations in leaf colour and size become more important than they would in better lit, more flowery surroundings. Among evergreens, some of the finest shrubs for handsome foliage are Japanese aucubas. Sadly, these plants have a somewhat sullied reputation, mainly because they are so often used where little else will grow. When healthy, however, and as long as the shade is not too dense, their foliage can be beautifully marked and has a high natural gloss. The tiny brown flowers are insignificant, but female plants provide a bonus of bright red berries. Good female varieties include the gold and green *A. japonica* 'Crotonifolia' and brighter gold and green variegated 'Sulphurea Marginata', whose leaf edges are cream. The male 'Picturata' has golden leaf centres.

Where flowering plants are used, it is important to favour white or pale-coloured varieties if there is a choice, since these show up more readily in low light. For fragrance and flower, several of the mahonias tolerate both shade and dryness. Sweetest smelling of all is *Mahonia japonica* which produces long racemes in late winter, curved in gentle 'S'-shapes and bearing a double row of strongly fragrant, primrose-yellow flowers. The scent is very similar to that of lily-of-the-valley. Later, another evergreen, almost as sweet scented, is *Osmanthus delavayi*, with tiny white

flowers and small, glossy leaves which make a pleasant texture contrast with the prickly leaves of mahonia. Such deciduous shrubs as *Rubus spectabilis* or *Viburnum farreri* (syn. *V. fragrans*) also provide fragrant blooms for late winter and early spring.

Natural herbaceous companions to the evergreen shrubs are stinking hellebores (*Helleborus foetidus*). Despite the name, the pungent smell of these attractive plants is hardly noticeable, even when they are picked and brought indoors. The Wester Flisk Group has reddish stems and pewter-hued leaves. Some of the lesser periwinkles (*Vinca minor*) make very useful ground-cover plants for scrambling about between these hellebores. In the wild, periwinkle is blue, but the pretty white form 'Gertrude Jekyll' shows up well in

the gloom. The dusky-purple 'Atropurpurea' does not, but is charming anyway.

Dry shade conditions generally lack enough moisture for many of the natural woodlanders seen in A Woodland Scene (pages 112–115), but outstanding exceptions are the hardy cyclamen. These can grow in the densest shade, where the ground dries almost to powder in summer. The most indestructible is *C. hederifolium*, which has exquisitely pink or white, swept-back blooms in autumn. Since it is such a highly variable species, resulting in endlessly fascinating patterned marbling on the foliage, it can add a great deal of interest. The leaves emerge towards the end of the flowering season and persist until the next summer. In winter, a few weeks after the very last of the autumn-blooming cyclamen have

faded, *C. coum* comes into flower, studding the ground with bright cerise flowers. The leaves are more rounded in shape than those of *C. hederifolium*, but many are well marbled and persist until the end of spring.

Massed bulbs give a sensational, albeit short, display. Where shade is dense, the bulbs may not survive very long, but by calling on the food reserves built up in their bulbs or corms, they will provide plenty of bright colour during their first couple of seasons. Tulips, especially white or pastel pink ones, pale-coloured hyacinths, white muscari and pale crocuses will all provide early joy. Such tropical beauties as hymenocallis or eucharis, can extend the colour into the next season, but these will survive outdoors only where winters are frost-free.

◄ A loquat (*Eriobotrya japonica*), the plant with the biggest leaves to the right, presides over a mixture of fruit-bearing *Mahonia japonica*, laurels and euonymus. All of these glossy evergreens thrive in dry shade, but the loquat is unlikely to bear fruit without any sunshine.

◄ The bold, leathery foliage of bergenias makes an enchanting contrast with the bright golden, glossy foliage of *Euonymus fortunei* Emerald 'n' Gold. The bergenia blossom is a spring bonus, and there is an evergreen cranesbill (*Geranium macrorrhizum*) to ensure continuity for the summer.

Windswept and coastal sites

Constant exposure to wind, salt and sand makes a coastal site very challenging for the gardener, but despite such unpromising conditions much can be achieved.

When planning a seaside garden, it is important that the outline planting doubles as a windbreak, creating a microclimate within. Trees such as the fast-growing columnar Monterey cypress (*Cupressus macrocarpa*) and the rounded Monterey pine (*Pinus radiata*) are impervious to wind. The former can be planted densely for use as windbreak hedging, but other excellent plants for this purpose are sea buckthorn (*Hippophae rhamnoides*), a gnarled, spiny shrub with grey-green foliage and masses of orange berries in the autumn, and *Griselinia littoralis*, an excellent evergreen hedging plant. Where strong winds prevail, a good hedge is better than a solid wall or fence since it allows air to filter through, reducing its force. A solid barrier causes the wind to eddy over the top, often resulting in damaging air turbulence on the other side.

Once a shelter is in place, the choice of smaller plants for the interior will widen. Among bright summer flowers, some species thrive especially well in coastal gardens. Members of the Livingstone daisy family, in particular lampranthus, mesembryanthemum and carpobrotus, give months of colour, as do portulacas and many of the smaller, fleshier sedums. *Sedum spathulifolium* 'Cape Blanco' is a particular beauty, with tight rosettes of purplish fleshy leaves overlaid with a smoky blue-grey covering, like a bloom.

Sea spray carried on the wind can increase potential damage to plants, particularly those that are sensitive to salt. Fortunately, there are a large number of species which not only tolerate salty conditions, but actually relish

▶ A subtropical effect has been achieved on this windy, coastal garden by planting the dubiously hardy *Beschorneria yuccoides*, ginger lilies (*Hedychium*) and other succulents. In a cold climate, most of these would need winter protection.

◄ In an upland setting, the stone wall gives but limited protection, since wind currents are likely to eddy over the top. Grasses are perfect for such a position – moving beautifully in wind and impervious to rough treatment. Here, colour is provided by the equally tough *Sedum spectabile*.

An open prairie planting

Meadow gardens can be as beautiful in open, windy sites as in sheltered gardens. Indeed, an exposed position will often help to keep meadow grasses and plants low and compact, making them less likely to collapse after wet weather. Although only two plants are featured here, it should be possible to grow an interesting range of wildflowers, such as spiny restharrow (*Ononis spinosa*), wild cranesbills (*Geranium pratense* or *G. sanguineum*) and any of the centaureas. Conditions will dictate which kinds do best: go for self-perpetuating perennials and avoid flashy, fast-growing annuals like cornflowers and poppies.

Plants' special needs

Establishment is easiest on very poor soils, planting mature plants in groups, rather than simply scattering seed. Management can be challenging, mainly because it is difficult to decide when to cut the grass, and when to leave it to grow. It is important to allow as many plants to seed as possible, so leave the mowings to wither and shed seed, but then rake them off and dispose of them elsewhere. Avoid invasive weeds such as docks and thistles since these could overrun desirable plants.

Others to try

On damp meadows, try ragged robin, (*Lychnis flos-cuculi*) and perhaps king cups (*Caltha palustris*). On very dry chalkland, or free-draining soil, try bird's foot trefoil (*Lotus corniculatus*) and harebells (*Campanula rotundifolia*).

Off-season echoes

For spring, try cowslips, daisies, snakeshead fritillaries, crocuses, salad burnet and snowdrops. For autumn, add in some colchicums or autumn-flowering crocuses such as *C. speciosus*.

them, and these, obviously, should be sought out. The sea buckthorn performs better near the sea than inland, for example, as do sea lavender (*Limonium*), feathery tamarisk and the leathery-leaved *Griselinia littoralis*. Plants that tolerate both salt and wind well include bupleurums, hebes, senecios, erigerons, red valerian and escallonias.

In cold climates, the sea has a moderating influence on winter temperatures. When frost grips inland regions, temperatures along the coastal strip may not fall to 0°C (32°F). This widens the range of plants that can be grown in seaside gardens. Marginally hardy plants such as *Fuchsia magellanica*, pampas grasses (*Cortaderia*) and the Chusan palm (*Trachycarpus fortunei*), an evergreen plant with large pleated leaves, have become associated with the coastal towns of countries whose interiors would be far too cold to sustain them.

◄ Ox-eye daisies (*Leucanthemum vulgare*) naturalized in a meadow with the rusty red-brown flowers of sheep sorrel.

Hot and dry areas

▲ A fresh, green mixture of drought-resistant plants cools down a hot, dry, free-draining gravel soil planting. Bergenias provide strong early colour which will be replaced by the pink of the sedums behind. The spiky, variegated century plant (*Agave americana*) will need winter protection.

Opportunities for successful planting on arid sites are immense, as a there is a large choice of plants deriving from desert or semi-arid areas all around the world. And as these regions can be cold as well as hot, or even experience huge fluctuations in temperature, a vast number of these drought-tolerant plants will survive cold winters.

Many plants have adapted to climatic extremes by 'going to ground' when the going gets tough. They survive by storing food in underground organs, then dying back until growth conditions once again become favourable. Although the storage organs may be bulbs, corms or tubers, these geophytes, as they are known by botanists, are often collectively known as 'bulbs'. For the dry garden, there is an unlimited choice of so-called bulbs to brighten every season, from winter beauties like snowdrops to such spring-flowering species as anemones, tulips and crocuses. Alliums, tigridias, albucas, galtonias and gladiolus flower in summer, and are followed by an enchanting autumn flush of colchicums, sternbergias and cyclamens. All of these can be used either in small groups as focal plants, or in drifts as a more general part of the understorey (see pages 36–39).

For outline planting, drought-tolerant shrubs tend to have silvery or grey foliage. In addition to those mentioned in Water-saving Garden (pages 146–147), all of which are suitable for planting in a hot, dry situation, the

◀ In late summer, the silvery foliage of *Stachys byzantina* makes a clear contrast with the darker, fleshier foliage of the sedums behind. These will retain their colour for several months, and even after they have died, they will present a handsome winter outline.

▶ A mix of succulents and rocks sustains interest in an autumn garden, even though it may not have rained for months. The tall grassy *Cyperus involucratus*, a water plant, is growing in a pond which is out of sight.

▼ Admirably complemented by red pelargoniums, the vigorous climber *Campsis radicans* furnishes a building in a Mediterranean-style planting. At ground level, osteospermums, a shrubby bugloss (*Echium*) and cordylines complete the charming collection.

shrubby brachyglottis (commonly known as senecio), which carries such bright yellow flowers, is a good choice. Less hardy, but also with gorgeous golden daisies are euryops and closely related argyranthemums. The thorny green stems of the hardy citrus poncirus provide sinister interest in winter, while its fragrant blossoms are a delight in summer. Even more sinister and thorny, but also rather shapely, is *Colletia paradoxa*. Instead of leaves, this has peculiar flattened processes along the stems, which remain green all winter and are covered with tiny white flowers in autumn.

Originally, such summer bedding as petunias, pelargoniums and, to a lesser extent, nasturtiums were considered almost drought-proof. Sophisticated breeding has changed their characters somewhat, but blending the older, small-flowered petunia varieties with marigolds or the wild-looking, single-flowered tagetes can create a hotly colourful effect. It is not always easy to find the older varieties, but such series as the weatherproof *Petunia* 'Polo Mixed' and some of the small-flowered trailing kinds like *P.* 'Million Bells' are almost as good. Some of the verbenas are fairly drought-tolerant, as are the more deep rooted of the tobaccos (*Nicotiana*). The latter wilt by day, but in the evening they revive, filling the air with sweet, heavy fragrance. *N. sylvestris*, a huge deep-rooted species, withstands drought surprisingly well, as can the closely related *Datura inoxia* (syn. *D. meteloides*). Among modern seed

strains of tobaccos, *N.* 'Fragrant Cloud' is a good choice. Although the pure white flowers wilt slightly during the heat of the day, they make up for this with sweet evening fragrance from midsummer to early autumn.

Never overlook the delight of seemingly vagrant annuals dotted about an arid planting. The occasional red poppy or larkspur, in blue, pink or white, the lovely Southern African heliophila, with cobalt-blue blooms, or even a monster like the giant thistle (*Onopordum nervosum*) can help to provide a planting with unexpected delight.

Heavy or chalky soil

Plants for problem soils

Heavy
Aster ericoides

Inula magnifica

Ligularia dentata

Malva moschata alba

Rosa 'Marguerite Hilling'

Rosa 'Nevada'

Chalky
Campanula lactiflora

Crataegus tanacetifolia

Dianthus

Malus tschonoskii

Roscoea cautleyoides 'Kew Beauty'

Problem soil can cause anxiety until you realize that no soil, not even the finest on earth, is without its particular problems. The two most important courses of action to take are to select plants most suited to the soil and to do whatever you can to minimize the effects of the problem. It also pays to observe which plants grow well in neighbouring gardens with similar soils. You might be very pleasantly surprised by what thrives in even the most awkward of sites, and in the hands of the most amateurish of gardeners.

Although heavy soils are slow to drain, cold and can be very difficult to work, they retain mineral nutrients for much longer than many other soils and are therefore almost always higher in fertility. Once plants are established in a heavy soil, they will then grow lustily. Improving drainage is important: incorporate grit, bonfire ash, road sweepings or anything that is likely to open up the soil and make it generally more crumbly. If feasible, installing a simple pipe drainage system to carry water away will greatly improve matters.

One of the main problems with heavy soils is that pressure compacts them, pushing the soil particles together, damaging the structure and reducing the rate at which water drains through. So it is sensible to walk on a heavy soil as little as possible, to protect it from pounding rain by laying organic mulches on the surface, and to improve the quality of the soil by incorporating mulches into the top few centimetres.

In times of drought, heavy soils often crack, especially where new planting has taken place. Pouring coarse sand or grit into the cracks reduces drying out. It also improves drainage, because as the cracks begin to close the next time it rains, as the wet soil swells, the sand remains in place, creating a drainage system.

Outline trees are easy to find for clays, from mighty hornbeams, which are lovely in the flame-like, fastigiate form as well as the normal spreading shape, to smaller crab apples, cherries and those smaller relatives of horse chestnuts, the buckeyes. Most cotoneasters, especially *C. lacteus* and *C. frigidus*, grow readily into small, shapely trees, as do some of the smaller of the willows. *Salix daphnoides* and *S. irrorata* are both pretty when cut hard back each spring, to encourage them to develop thick brushes of young stems that will be decorated with silvery catkins in late winter.

Among understorey plants, roses adore heavy ground, flowering more profusely and for longer than on less fertile soil. Clematis too, are happy in clays, especially alkaline clays, and therefore make superb companions for the roses.

Tall perennials such as *Inula magnifica* grow so vast on clay, that they become architectural features. *Crambe cordifolia*, gunneras and rheums and are all tall growing. There is also a wide choice of small perennials that cope well with clay. Cowslips and primroses are happy on heavy soil, as are the burnets, cranesbills and other meadowland flowers. Meadow cranesbill (*Geranium pratense*) is lovely in its pure wild state, but such garden forms as the blue-streaked lavender-grey *G*. 'Mrs Kendall

Clark' or the double 'Plenum Violaceum' (syn. 'Flore Pleno') are almost as pretty.

Thin soil that overlies pure chalk is very hungry, quick to dry out and can, in extreme conditions, erode away, leaving the bare chalk in which very little will grow. The second problem with chalky soil is its alkalinity: lime-hating plants such as heathers, camellias, rhododendrons and azaleas cannot survive in it. Fortunately, there are plenty of beautiful lime-loving plants, including daphnes, burnet roses, hypericums, pinks and carnations, to choose from. In the wild, chalkland supports a fascinating and colourful understorey of plants, most 'of which have the added advantage of being drought-resistant. In shade, grow stinking hellebore (*Helleborus foetidus*), wild orchids and the evergreen *Iris foetidissima*, which has wonderful autumn fruits, as well as colchicums and campanulas.

Outline trees that thrive on chalk include hawthorns, which grow nicely gnarled and characterful in poor growing conditions. The wild spindle tree (*Euonymus europaeus*) is another good choice. Although its summer flowers are inconspicuous, the curiously shaped fruits open in autumn to reveal their seed. The clone 'Red Cascade' has magnificent red autumn foliage and startling pink and orange fruits.

▼The giant thistle (*Onopordum nervosum*) soars to almost 3m (10ft) in a single growing season, and, though happy on any soil, it will always grow larger and more dramatic on heavy soil. Here, the purple blooms of *Allium hollandicum* (syn. *A. aflatunense*) make a pleasant foil for the huge silver-grey leaves of the thistle.

▲ A glorious contrast has been created on a vertical chalky site by blending two lime-tolerant plants – a yellow banksian rose (*Rosa banksiae* 'Lutea') with an early flowering Californian lilac (*Ceanothus*). The judicious selection of plants will ensure an excellent display on problems sites.

Page numbers in *italic* refer to the illustrations.

The publisher thanks the photographers and organizations for their kind permission to reproduce the following photographs in this book:

1 Georgia Glynn-Smith; 2-3 John Glover/Sticky Wicket, Dorchester, Dorset; 4-7 Georgia Glynn-Smith; 8 Charles Mann; 9 left Beatrice Pichon-Clarisse; 9 right Andrew Lawson /designer Ryl Nowell, Wilderness Farm, Sussex; 10-11 above Clive Nichols/Beth Chatto Garden, Essex; 10-11 below S&O Mathews; 11 David McDonald/PhotoGarden; 12-13 above Maggie Oster; 12-13 below Beatrice Pichon-Clarisse; 13 Noel Kavanagh; 14-15 above Derek St Romaine; 14-15 below Mark Bolton; 15 Andrew Lawson; 16-17 above S&O Mathews; 16-17 below Clive Nichols; 17 Jerry Harpur/Hadspen House, Somerset; 18 Anne Hyde; 18-19 David McDonald/PhotoGarden; 20-21 Andrew Lawson; 22 Jerry Harpur/Beth Chatto Garden, Essex; 22-23 Christine Ternynck; 23 Marianne Majerus/designer Mark Rumary; 24 Georgia Glynn-Smith; 24-25 Marianne Majerus; 26 Beatrice Pichon-Clarisse; 26-27 Jerry Harpur/Dolwen, Wales; 27 Andrew Lawson/Hermannshof, Weinheim, Germany; 28 Susan Witney; 28-29 Beatrice Pichon-Clarisse; 29 Andrew Lawson/The Old Rectory, Sudborough, Northants; 30 David McDonald/PhotoGarden/ gardener Mr Steven Antenow; 30-31 Andrew Lawson/The Garden House, Buckland Monachorum, Devon; 32 Mark Bolton/Sudeley Castle, Gloucestershire; 32-33 John Glover/Great Dixter; 33 above Andrew Lawson/Bosvigo House, Cornwall; 33 below Noel Kavanagh; 34 Jerry Harpur/Gravetye Manor, Sussex; 34-35 Jerry Harpur/design Joe Eck & Wayne Winterrowd, Vermont, USA; 35 Jerry Harpur/Westbury Court, Gloucestershire; 36 Andrew Lawson/Sticky Wicket, Dorchester, Dorset; 36-37 Andrew Lawson; 37 Mark Bolton/Sherbourne Garden, Somerset; 38-39 Maggie Oster/Noerenberg Memorial Gardens, Orono, Minnesota; 39 Andrew Lawson /designer Arne Maynard; 40 Georgia Glynn-Smith/Alan Gray & Graham Robeson; 40-41 above Beatrice Pichon-Clarisse/Festival des Jardins de Chaumont/Loire; 41 Georgia Glynn-Smith/Gill Richardson; 42 Andrew Lawson/Beth Chatto Gardens, Essex; 42-43 John Glover/Wollerton Old Hall; 43 Clive Nichols/The Garden House, Gloucestershire; 44 Anne Hyde; 44-45 Derek St Romaine/RHS Rosemoor Garden; 46-47 Maggie Oster/RHS Rosemoor Garden; 47 left Clive Nichols/Chenies Manor, Bucks; 47 right Beatrice Pichon-Clarisse; 48 Georgia Glynn-Smith/Alan Gray & Graham Robeson; 48-49 above Georgia Glynn-Smith/John Richardson; 48-49 below Noel Kavanagh; 49 Derek St Romaine; 50 Jerry Harpur/Wyken Hall, Suffolk; 50-51 Jerry Harpur;

51 above S&O Mathews; 51 below Marianne Majerus; 52-53 Jerry Harpur/Heslington Manor, Yorkshire; 54-61 Georgia Glynn-Smith; except 56 far right Andrew Lawson; 62 left Clive Nichols; 62 right Noel Kavanagh; 63 left Clive Nichols; 63 centre Andrew Lawson; 63 right Andrew Lawson; 64-67 Georgia Glynn-Smith; 68-69 Georgia Glynn-Smith/Alan Gray & Graham Robeson; 70 Marianne Majerus; 71 above Georgia Glynn-Smith/Alan Gray & Graham Robeson; 71 below left Georgia Glynn-Smith/Alan Gray & Graham Robeson; 71 below right Andrew Lawson; 72-73 Georgia Glynn-Smith/Gill Richardson; 74 above Georgia Glynn-Smith/Gill Richardson; 74 below left Andrew Lawson; 74 below centre left Georgia Glynn-Smith/Gill Richardson; 74 below centre right Georgia Glynn-Smith/Gill Richardson; 74 below right Georgia Glynn-Smith/Gill Richardson; 74-75 Andrew Lawson; 75 Georgia Glynn-Smith/Gill Richardson; 76-77 Georgia Glynn-Smith/Anne Huntington; 77 Jerry Harpur; 79 above Georgia Glynn-Smith; 79 below Georgia Glynn-Smith/Anne Huntington; 80-81 Georgia Glynn-Smith/Anne Huntington; 82 John Glover; 82-83 Clive Nichols/The Priory, Kemerton, Worcestershire; 83 Clive Nichols/The Priory, Kemerton, Worcestershire; 84 left Andrew Lawson; 84 right Clive Nichols/The Priory, Kemerton, Worcestershire; 85 above left Clive Nichols; 85 above right John Glover; 85 below Clive Nichols/The Priory, Kemerton, Worcestershire; 86 left Clive Nichols; 86 right Georgia Glynn-Smith; 86-87 Georgia Glynn-Smith; 88 left Andrew Lawson; 88 right Clive Nichols; 89 Georgia Glynn-Smith; 90 Garden Picture Library/Joan Dear; 90-91 Jerry Harpur /designers Mary Effron & Javier Valdivia, Santa Monica, California; 91 Andrew Lawson; 92 left Andrew Lawson; 92 right Clive Nichols/Architectural Plants, Sussex; 93 left Andrew Lawson; 93 centre left Clive Nichols; 93 centre right Andrew Lawson; 93 right Garden Picture Library/Jerry Pavia; 94-97 John Glover/Beechcroft Road; 98 John Glover; 98-99 Jerry Harpur/Heslington Manor, Yorkshire; 99 S&O Mathews; 100 left Clive Nichols; 100 right Jerry Harpur; 101 above Jerry Harpur/Heslington Manor, Yorkshire; 101 below left Clive Nichols; 101 below centre S&O Mathews; 101 below right Andrew Lawson; 102-103 John Glover; 104-105 Clive Nichols/The Old Vicarage, Norfolk/designers Alan Gray & Graham Robeson; 106 left Georgia Glynn-Smith; 106 centre Clive Nichols; 106 right Clive Nichols; 107 left Georgia Glynn-Smith; 107 right

Clive Nichols/The Old Vicarage, Norfolk/designers Alan Gray & Graham Robeson; 108 Andrew Lawson; 108-109 Andrew Lawson/Gothic House, Oxfordshire; 109-111 Andrew Lawson; 112 S&O Mathews; 112-113 Andrew Lawson; 114 left Andrew Lawson; 114 right Clive Nichols; 115 above S&O Mathews; 115 below Andrew Lawson; 116-117 Georgia Glynn-Smith/Alan Gray & Graham Robeson; 118 left Georgia Glynn-Smith/Alan Gray & Graham Robeson; 118 right Clive Nichols; 119 below right Clive Nichols; 119 above, below left & below centre Georgia Glynn-Smith/Alan Gray & Graham Robeson; 120 S&O Mathews; 120-121 S&O Mathews; 121 above John Glover; 121 below Garden Picture Library/Jerry Pavia; 122 left Andrew Lawson; 122 right John Glover; 122-123 John Glover; 123 left Garden Picture Library/JS Sira; 123 right Garden Picture Library/Christopher Gallagher; 124-125 Georgia Glynn-Smith/Glynne & Rose Clay; 126 below left Andrew Lawson; 126 below right Clive Nichols; 126 above, below left, below centre & below right Georgia Glynn-Smith/Glynne & Rose Clay; 127 Georgia Glynn-Smith/Glynne & Rose Clay; 128-130 Georgia Glynn-Smith; 131 above, below centre & below right Georgia Glynn-Smith; 131 below left Clive Nichols; 132 Andrew Lawson; 132-133 S&O Mathews/North Court, Isle of Wight; 134-135 Maggie Oster; 135 left Georgia Glynn-Smith; 135 right S&O Mathews; 136 S&O Mathews; 137 above Derek St Romaine; 137 below S&O Mathews; 138 S&O Mathews; 138-139 Anne Hyde/Winslow Hall, Buckinghamshire; 139 Anne Hyde; 140-141 S&O Mathews; 142 Jerry Harpur/Designer Victor Nelson, New York; 143 left Jerry Harpur/designer Camille Muller, Paris; 143 right Marianne Majerus/designer Leslie Sayers; 144 Beatrice Pichon-Clarisse /Specker Nursery, France; 145 above S&O Mathews/Merrie Cottage, Hampshire; 145 below Mark Bolton/Batsford Arboretum; 146 Jerry Harpur/Beth Chatto Gardens, Essex; 147 above Andrew Lawson/Beth Chatto Gardens, Essex; 147 below Charles Mann; 148 Jerry Harpur/Andrew Weaving, London; 149 S&O Mathews/Beth Chatto Gardens, Essex; 150 John Glover/Overbecks, Devon, National Trust; 151 above Mark Bolton/designer Lesley Rosser; 151 below S&O Mathews; 152 Jerry Harpur/Beth Chatto Gardens, Essex; 153 above left Jerry Harpur/Beth Chatto Gardens, Essex; 153 above right Jerry Harpur/Dennis Lochen and Ted Chaffers, Spain; 153 below Andrew Lawson; 154-155 S&O Mathews/The White House, Sussex; 155 S&O Mathews.